Perpetuating TRUTH Through Teaching

CLANCY P. HAYES

Gospel Publishing House
Springfield, Missouri
02-0517

Unless otherwise indicated, Scripture is taken from the NEW AMERICAN STANDARD BIBLE®, copyright © 1960, 1962, 1963, 1968, 1971, 1972, 1973, 1975, 1977, 1995 by The Lockman Foundation. Used by permission. (www.lockman.org)

ISBN 0-88243-830-1

©2005 by Gospel Publishing House, Springfield, Missouri 65802-1894. All rights reserved. No part of this book may be reproduced, stored in a retrieval system, or transmitted in any form or by any means—electronic, mechanical, photocopy, recording, or otherwise—without prior written permission of the copyright owner, except brief quotations used in connection with reviews in magazines or newspapers.

Printed in the United States of America

Contents

Introduction		5
1	Perpetuating Truth Through **Faithfulness**	7
2	Perpetuating Truth Through **Authenticity**	27
3	Perpetuating Truth Through **Compassion**	45
4	Perpetuating Truth Through **Leadership**	65
5	Perpetuating Truth Through **Involvement**	85
6	Perpetuating Truth Through **Conviction**	105
7	Perpetuating Truth Through **Relationship**	125
8	Perpetuating Truth Through **Instruction**	145

Introduction

" 'Heaven and earth will pass away, but My words will not pass away' " (Matthew 24:35).

" 'Upon this rock I will build My church; and the gates of Hades will not overpower it' " (Matthew 16:18).

"The Church is just one generation from extinction."

"God has no grandchildren."

Most of us have heard these quotes or similar ones. We can sense the tension between Jesus' confidence in declaring what He knows to be true about the future of the Church and the caution of those who realize that the fate of the Church, to a great extent, has been left in the hands of mortals.

When Jesus ascended into heaven, He left a handful of people to perpetuate the truth He had actualized while on earth. Those individuals did not have the luxury of keeping their faith to themselves. If they had done so, Jesus' work would have been short-circuited.

Thankfully, Jesus' early followers spread His message of love and forgiveness to their community and beyond. In a relatively short period of time, people throughout the then-known world had heard the gospel and in many cases embraced it. Just four hundred years after a ragtag group of unknowns were commissioned to "go into all the world" (Mark 16:15), Christianity became the prominent religion in the world.

The success of Christianity hasn't been by accident. Individual effort, combined with the power of the Holy Spirit, has led to millions of people accepting Jesus as Savior. These efforts were intentional and purposeful. One by one the kingdom of God has grown, and Jesus' confidence in His followers has been rewarded. Those who have gone before us have passed the baton well, but we must not be content to celebrate their success. It is our turn to pass the baton to the next generation.

This book is designed to help you do two things: (1) make a successful transference of your faith by examining how our predecessors transmitted their faith and (2) glean valuable skills that will make you successful in accomplishing your task. The Bible presents a variety of excellent examples to help us perpetuate the faith that has been entrusted to us.

Teachers have been assigned one of the most important roles in the church, and the Bible tells us they are worthy of "double honor" (1 Timothy 5:17). James informs us that teachers will be held to a higher level of accountability (James 3:1). Your role as a teacher of God's Word is not taken lightly by God, and it must not be taken lightly by you.

My hope is that you will find your journey through this book delightful. As we revisit familiar biblical narratives, I hope you will see yourself in the place of these famous teachers and leaders. As you witness individuals building their faith on the faith of their forefathers, I hope you will continually be reminded of those who have invested in your life and will express appreciation to God for their faithful witness. And most of all, I pray that your work will stand the test of time as you do your part to ensure that the body of Christ grows stronger until the day Jesus returns to claim His bride.

Clancy P. Hayes

CHAPTER 1

Perpetuating Truth Through **Faithfulness**

*God calls us, not to success,
but to faith—obedience and trust
and service—and He bids us to be
unconcerned with measuring the
merits of our work the way
the world does. We are to sow;
He will reap as He pleases.*

~ *Charles Colson*

A lone figure stood looking over his fields. He smiled as he watched the heads of grain blow in the wind. The man took the brilliant sunshine for granted because he had never experienced a day when the sun did not appear, but he was thankful for the blessings its rays provided.

Overall, life had been good to him. He had found a lovely wife. She was all he could have asked for and more. Her clear skin and sparkling eyes were a pleasure to look at each morning. Her inner beauty was even more appealing. She had given him three fine sons and made do with what she had to provide him a home anyone would envy.

Like any other man of his day, he faced the challenges of raising a family and keeping food on the table, but he was thankful to his God for the life he had. Each morning he walked out to his fields to start his day by watching the dew evaporate into the air while giving thanks to his God for all He had done for him.

As the man's sons began to transition into manhood, he became increasingly concerned about their spiritual future. He had come from a long line of individuals who believed in one true God and sought ways to serve Him. But life was different these days. Fewer and fewer people in his community believed there was only one God, let alone served Him. His oldest son had started to spend time with a friend whose family ridiculed those who believed in God. His middle son just last week had asked why his father spent so much of his day talking to a God no one could see. Fortunately, the youngest had not begun to challenge the family faith, but the father knew it probably would be only a matter of time before he did.

That night after the boys had gone to bed, the man sat down with his wife and shared his concerns. She was well aware of the change that had begun to take place in society but had not given a great deal of thought to its impact on her boys. He and his wife prayed to their God and asked for direction regarding what they could do to ensure that their faith would be perpetuated in their boys' lives.

The answer they received was clear and simple. God told them to live out their faith before their sons by being totally obedient to Him. They agreed without realizing the consequences this commitment would bring.

On yet another clear and bright morning, Noah stood out by his fields thinking about his God and his boys. But this day would be like no other, for it was on this day that God told Noah that He was going to send rain on the earth. God went on to tell him that the rain would continue for forty days and that it was Noah's responsibility to share this message with his family and the other people with whom he lived and to build a boat big enough to house anyone who wanted to get inside.

This information was difficult for Noah to comprehend. The concept of rain was outside his realm of understanding, and the idea of a big boat seemed preposterous. But then he remembered his commitment to God to be obedient to Him in the eyes of his sons. Noah decided he would make an attempt to live according to his convictions.

That evening Noah gathered his family around him and told them about his encounter with God. You could see the humiliation on Ham's face as he thought about his reputation in town when people caught wind of this. Shem's sarcastic remarks were even more cutting than Noah could have expected. Japheth just sat and wondered what his dad was talking about.

After their conversation, Noah wondered if he had done more harm than good to his family's faith by revealing this information. If Noah had not been convinced that the instructions had been from God, he would have told them he was mistaken. But he couldn't. He knew God's voice and would live in obedience to God's commands in spite of the ridicule he and his family would face.

Day after day Noah labored under the hot sun gathering wood for the boat. Year after year Noah endured the inquisitive looks and the ridicule of those who passed by as the ship began to take shape. Each time Noah told the people about the Flood that would destroy the earth, people told him that he was a fool and that his God was laughable. And the three developing young men watched their father live in accordance with the truth he proclaimed in spite of the consequences.

Gaining Perspective

A common thread that weaves all followers of God together throughout time is our uniqueness within society. Noah lived among the people of his community but stood apart from them because of his beliefs. For well over one hundred years, Noah went about his countercultural lifestyle as a testimony of his faith in his God.

When the floodwaters finally broke forth from the sky, only Noah's family and the prescribed animals were aboard the ark. Years of lifestyle evangelism yielded what seemed to be very little reward. The cries of thousands gasping for their last breath as the waters engulfed them must have rung in Noah's ears from that day forward. It is quite possible that Noah questioned God concerning His wisdom and wondered about the future as he and his family stood alone as the only humans who remained on the earth.

Noah must have experienced a mixed set of emotions over the days between the first drops of rain and the moment the ark settled on dry ground. But two things were clear in his mind: God is faithful to His Word, and He rewards those who obey Him. This was a truth Noah embraced and transmitted to his children, and it has been perpetuated throughout the years to all who will hear and believe.

Today, as believers in the one true God, we too hold beliefs that are scoffed at by many in our society. God may not call us to build a boat in the middle of a desert, but He often calls us to do things just as radical. Our society tells us to act in a selfish manner, but God tells us to be willing to give all we possess (Matthew 19:21). Our society tells us to exercise our rights, but God tells us to forgive and to show mercy (Matthew 18:21,22). Our society looks for pleasure through indulgences of the flesh, but God tells us to take up our cross daily (Luke 9:23). Those who follow God's directives look a great deal like Noah and receive much the same reaction by onlookers who ridicule. This should not surprise us. The apostle Paul told the Corinthians that the very nature of the gospel is seen as foolishness by those who do not have spiritual insight (1 Corinthians 1:18).

Noah stood firm in his faith despite the challenges he faced. He could have buckled under the pressure and compromised. He could have walked away from the ark and invested his time in good works of another kind. He probably would have been rewarded by his culture for such a decision. But if he had done so, he and his family would have joined the others in a sea of death when God poured out His judgment on the earth, and the truth of God would not have been perpetuated.

As teachers of the gospel, we have been asked to proclaim God's truth to this generation. We will face many challenges as we attempt to faithfully discharge our duties. It is vital that we follow Noah's example of faithfulness even in those times when compromise would be much easier.

Noah's life and ministry provide some important principles we can adopt to help us become more effective as we minister to others in a culture that stands in opposition to our faith.

Gleaning Principles

1. Be a Part of Our Community

Can you imagine what it must have been like to be Noah? As he went about his ministry of ark building, the people of his community snickered, little children stared, and the brash made fun of him and his God. Such a ministry environment was probably very uncomfortable for Noah.

Noah could have chosen to move outside of his community to build the ark. His life probably would have been a lot easier if he had isolated himself from the pagan community, but he chose to remain in his community and conduct his ministry in full view of his detractors.

As Christians, we have been called to perform our ministries in full view of our communities. As in Noah's community, many in our communities do not understand God's ways and make it very uncomfortable for us to perform our ministries. Just as Noah endured laughter and ridicule, we will likely experience opposition when we construct the "arks" God calls us to build.

Some Sunday School teachers have chosen to isolate themselves from their communities. They feel that it is safer to stay inside the walls of the church to perform their ministries. They are satisfied to hold their classes, sing their songs, and live their faith among the faithful. But when they do this, those for whom the "ark" was designed never get a chance to see it. The ministries of the church become inbred and have little effect on those who need them the most. Churches and Sunday School classes that are effective are ones whose leaders and participants are not afraid of living as peculiar people among a lost world.

Effective ministries find ways to take the gospel to the lost so the light of the gospel can be seen in the darkness (Matthew 5:14–16). We must never be afraid to live within our culture and our communities. Jesus taught that the gospel was primarily designed for the spiritually sick, not for those who are well (Matthew 9:12). The gospel is the medicine people in our culture need, whether they know it or not. It is our responsibility to make the medicine available to all who will receive it.

Is it possible that Sunday School teachers are instrumental in creating sinners in the process of doing their teaching ministry? The apostle James wrote, "To one who knows the right thing to do and does not do it, to him it is sin" (James 4:17). Could it be that if we teach people what God wants them to accomplish through their lives yet fail to offer opportunities to carry out these demands in practical ways, we are causing them to commit sins of omission?

Each individual is responsible to find ways to fulfill God's will for his or her life, but teachers can provide avenues to help them accomplish this. One way is to encourage our students to become actively involved in ministries to those outside the church.

What can you and your class do to make your ministry more visible in your community? Are you willing to risk the embarrassment, ridicule, and pain that may come through this type of exposure in order to perpetuate the truth in the community in which God has placed you?

2. Present a Clear Message in the Midst of the Culture

Noah's message to his community was clear. He told his neighbors that God was going to send a flood and that they could avoid destruction if they would enter the ark he was building. The people refused to accept the message because it didn't fit into their philosophical constructs. Since they had never seen a drop of rain, it just didn't make sense that there would be a flood. Noah's message of destruction seemed preposterous to a culture that had been free to do whatever it wished without consequences. Even those who might have believed Noah at first began to have doubts after the first twenty or thirty years passed with no sign of the judgment he predicted.

As teachers, we too must present a clear message. We live in a culture much like the one in which Noah found himself. People today have a difficult time accepting the fact that there is only one way to heaven. The Cross seems as useless to this generation as the ark did to Noah's generation. Few really believe that God will bring judgment on those who sin against Him. And considering the length of time that has passed since the promise was given, even some Christians begin to doubt Christ's promise to return. But just as with the Flood in Noah's day, God will fulfill all the promises He has made in His Word. Our job is to proclaim those promises regardless of how foolish that may seem to others.

3. Act According to Your Convictions

If Noah had proclaimed that a flood was coming but neglected to pick up a hammer, he would have had very little impact. Noah demonstrated his belief in his message by acting according to it. Each day he proclaimed the message of God through both his words and deeds.

Declaring God's truth through the presentation of our lessons each week is essential for Sunday School teachers. And equally important is living the truth we proclaim in front of our students and in our communities each day. Our culture, as well as that of our students, demands authenticity when it comes to spiritual matters. Too many people have seen spiritual leaders declare the truths of the Bible and then get caught in the very sins they condemned. People have very little tolerance for hypocrisy. If you are going to accept the responsibility to teach, you must understand that you will be held to a higher standard (James 3:1).

Living according to your convictions doesn't mean that you have to be perfect. It simply means that you must be honest with your challenges and be willing to let your students see you rely on God for strength and help as you attempt to live according to the standards God has declared in Scripture. You must be willing to forgive, repent, trust, and live a life of holy commitment to God. In other words, you must take the message of the Bible seriously.

4. Leave the Results With God

Noah must have been greatly disappointed when God closed the door of the ark and only his family and the animals were on board. A lifetime of ministry and only a handful of people were affected by his efforts.

Many teachers become discouraged because their Sunday School classes are small. They work faithfully to prepare lessons, they pray for their students, and they stand in their classrooms week after week, but the results of their ministry seem very small in comparison to what they could be. These individuals can relate to Noah.

If the story had ended on the day the door of the ark closed, Noah might have had reason to feel disappointed. But the story did not end there. The impact of Noah's life of faithfulness continues to this day. When Noah and his family got off the ark, they made a sacrifice and continued to minister. New generations filled the earth. God's truth was proclaimed to them, and some accepted it and lived according to it. If Noah had not been faithful to build the ark, he too would have been lost in the flood, and the truth of God would have stopped at that point.

Noah didn't see the full impact of his ministry in his lifetime, and neither will we. It is our responsibility to be faithful to the ministry to which God has called us and leave the results with Him. We can look back on Noah's life and draw strength and hope that we are making a difference that will perpetuate the truth throughout time even when the evidence around us seems to say something quite different.

Giving It a Try

1. Making a Contribution to Our Communities

A church in Aurora, Colorado, has come up with an ingenious way to get their people to reach out to their community. Each quarter every class is required to do an outreach project. Each week the pastor shows a video clip of a class outreach to the congregation to encourage others to get involved and celebrate their obedience to God by ministering to their community.

A church in the Los Angeles area has converted a hospital into a ministry center that is open twenty-four hours a day, seven days a week. This did not happen by chance. The young pastor chose to reach out to the gang-ridden neighborhood, and God blessed his efforts. If he had remained isolated inside the doors of the church, the "ark" God designed for him to build would not have been built. The church and its educational groups continue to spread the love of God to the community through weekly block outreaches.

Your community holds many similar opportunities for service. Men in the adult classes might offer a free oil change to single mothers, women might offer a "mother's day out," teens might do a free car wash or offer to mow lawns in a neighborhood. Children could visit nursing homes and bring joy to the patients. The possibilities are endless, but the secret is to get started and to view your service as ministry.

The key is to help your students see the need to live among unbelievers and overcome any fear and prejudice they have toward the lost. Your task is to help them see that lifestyle evangelism is a natural expression of the love God has instilled in them. Reaching out into a hostile environment is a risk each of us is called to take.

2. Getting the People's Attention

The noise of building an ark got the attention of Noah's audience. Each time a person walked by the ever-growing boat, he or she was confronted with the truth. As teachers, we must likewise get the attention of our audience in a clear and precise manner.

We are kidding ourselves if we think we can get the attention of people in this culture by using means we used thirty-five years ago. There was a time when the filmstrip and recorder were state-of-the-art media that caught people's attention, but this is no longer the case. Neither can we expect to attract them by doing Sunday School as we have always done it. One person once said the definition of insanity is to continue to do the same things in the same ways and then to expect different results. If we want our culture to hear us, we must we willing to try new things.

In the book *Give Them What They Want: Turning Sunday School Into a Place People Want to Be,* the authors identify eight felt needs all people have.[1] They say that Sunday Schools that seek to build relationships, provide a sense of purpose, provide a place of acceptance, help people encounter God, present a clear message of truth, help people learn a better way to live, provide an enjoyable environment, and answer questions people are asking will catch people's attention. If your class addresses these needs in an effective manner, people will be attracted to your class. Practical strategies for making your Sunday School an attractive place can be gained from this important resource, which is available through Gospel Publishing House.

3. Being Willing to Be Transparent

Teachers should never teach a lesson they are not willing to respond to individually. It is the height of hypocrisy to expect our students to respond to a message to which we are not willing to respond. This is not to say that we must have perfectly achieved the spiritual discipline being presented. It is simply to say that we must be willing to share personal struggles with the issue and be willing to trust God to help us live obediently.

A delicate balance exists between being transparent and being overexposed. Our students don't need to know the dirty little details of our lives any more than we need to know theirs. But they do need to know that we are not perfect and that we struggle just as they struggle. We need to share with them how God provides strength and hope in our lives so that they can have hope in their difficult times. And they need to know the strategies we have used to grow deeper in our relationship with God so that they can imitate us as we imitate Christ (1 Corinthians 11:1).

Noah's family saw him up close and personal. They could have run away from home and joined the crowd, but because they saw the consistency of his life, they stood by his side. Your students will learn more about God by watching your life than they will ever learn by listening to your words. Don't miss this important teaching opportunity.

4. Trusting God With the Results

All of us would like to have more students and better spiritual results in exchange for the effort we expend. We would like to see each of our students growing in Christ, reading the Bible each day, and reaching the masses for Christ, but few of us experience these results. This can be frustrating if we don't keep things in perspective. Remember that God has only given you the responsibility to minister and care for the people He has entrusted to you. It is their responsibility to respond to God.

Instead of focusing on your results, focus on your students' needs. Pray for them each day. Call them and talk with them about things that are important to them. Love your students through fellowship and assistance in their areas of need. Put as much energy into preparing your lesson if you have one student as you would if you had one hundred in your class.

Consider the potential of each student in your class and the possible spiritual fruit that could spring from just one of their lives. Give thanks to God for the faithful servants who have invested in your life to allow you to have the opportunity to invest in the lives of your students.

God has a plan to perpetuate His truth, and He has selected you to be an important part of that plan. As you faithfully execute your duties, God will be faithful to bring His plan to fruition. You can rejoice in this truth and rest assured that future generations will be blessed because of the work you are doing in the community in which He has placed you.

It Works

Two young friends were playing. One of the boys came from a traditional home with a father who worked in the post office and a mother who stayed home. This young boy went to church and Sunday School each week. The other boy came from a broken home. The stepfather and mother were problem drinkers and on the verge of divorce. This boy had never seen the inside of a church. Although from different worlds, the boys learned to enjoy each other's company.

One day the boy who attended Sunday School asked his friend if he would like to attend. The Sunday School was having a contest and had encouraged students to invite their friends, so Peter did. His unchurched friend agreed to attend to help Peter win the prize that was being offered to the person who brought the most friends to Sunday School.

When the visitor entered the church for the first time, he noticed the atmosphere was different than he had ever experienced before. The adults there looked like they were having fun. There was no beer and no cigarette smoke. There was no yelling, no name calling, and no one seemed afraid.

When the boy got to class, the teacher seemed glad to see him. There were interesting things to do. He gained approval and was treated nicely. And he learned a great deal that first day. Probably the most important thing he learned was that Jesus loved him so much that He died for him. The teacher clearly declared that the boy needed to be forgiven of his sins and needed to ask Jesus to be the leader of his life. The boy listened and believed.

In the following weeks, the boy shared his Sunday School experiences with his parents. He begged them to come to church because he knew it would help them. The parents finally decided to go to church on a Sunday evening just to quiet their young son's pleadings. That night the parents heard a clear presentation of the gospel and accepted Jesus as Savior. Their lives were transformed, and they resolved their marital issues and continued to attend the same church together for more than forty years.

The teacher who led the boy to Christ could not have imagined the difference he made in that family, the church, and the larger church community. You see, the family stayed intact and prevented a young boy and his siblings from having to go through another set of struggles that only walking down that road would have revealed. The church was positively impacted because the mother of the young boy became an effective evangelist to those with whom she worked. People who knew her past could not have ignored the difference Christ had made in her life. That provided her with an open door to share the gospel, and many took the opportunity to walk through that door. And the young boy grew up to become a minister, a teacher, and a writer of curriculum and training materials. As a matter of fact, you are being influenced right now by that Sunday School teacher's efforts and the courage of a boy to reach out to his friend. I was the boy who was introduced to the gospel and responded to it.

The Rest of the Story

Noah's sons could not shake their father's commitment to his boat project. They had watched him before his supposed encounter with God and had trusted his judgment then. They determined that he had either truly heard from God or had gone mad. But outside of this zany activity, he was the same person they had always known.

Slowly the boys' disdain for their dad shifted to admiration. His faith was unlike the faith of others in the community who claimed to serve a "god." Their lives were inconsistent. They served their gods when it was convenient. When things weren't as they desired, they simply adjusted their god to fit their faith or ignored their god's demands; but not Dad. For years he had stayed faithful to his belief even when everyone encouraged him to quit.

One day Japheth picked up one of his father's tools and walked up beside him and asked if he could help. Japheth had always been the most agreeable child, and it warmed Noah's heart that at least one of his sons might perpetuate the family's faith. Soon Ham and Shem were working alongside their dad as well. And the boat project soon became a family affair as Noah's wife and his daughters-in-law brought cool drinks and food to the men as they labored into the night.

On the day the rains began, Noah had mixed emotions. He wished everyone he had warned would have come aboard the ark, but a sense of satisfaction filled him as he looked at each member of his family sitting dry inside. God had been faithful to Noah, and his faith had been successfully passed on.

Conclusion

Although many don't know it, our world needs Jesus. Only when they have experienced the love of Jesus personally will they fully understand (1 Corinthians 2:14,15). Until that time, we must continue to stand in their midst and pound the nails into the ark that He has called us to build.

It is tempting to look at our task and wonder if it is worth the effort for the results we are seeing, but remember that you seldom see the full extent of the fruit of your labor immediately.

God's love was extended to humankind in the creation, and has continued throughout the ages one generation at a time. At times it seemed that the message was going to die out, but God always found at least one faithful servant to keep the message alive.

In our generation, you have been called to keep God's message alive. As you plant seeds of God's Word into the lives of your students, you are investing in the future. You are following in the footsteps of many faithful servants of God in the past. And you will share in the eternal rewards that await all those who have participated in the perpetuation of God's truth to those who need to gather into God's ark of protection.

Personal Reflection

1. What are your greatest struggles in continuing to be faithful to your call as a teacher, and how has this chapter helped address those issues?
2. What do you do now to attract students' attention, and what can you do to enhance this area of your teaching ministry?
3. Who are some people who have made an impact on your life, and how can you communicate your appreciation to these people?

4. What steps can you take to become more student-centered in your approach to teaching rather than focusing on your own accomplishments as a teacher?

[1]Michael H. Clarensau and Clancy P. Hayes, *Give Them What They Want: Turning Sunday School Into a Place People Want To Be* (Springfield, Mo.: Gospel Publishing House, 2001).

CHAPTER 2

Perpetuating Truth Through **Authenticity**

Do not think about your character. If you will think about what you ought to do for other people, your character will take care of itself. Character is a by-product, and any man who devotes himself to its cultivation in his own case will become a selfish prig.

~ Woodrow Wilson

An elderly man sat in his home admiring all he had acquired over his lifetime. He had a great wife, a fabulous home, and more servants than the average rancher. He truly had been blessed. His greatest joy, however, was watching his son work in the fields. Oh, how thankful he was to have had the opportunity to watch his child grow into a fine young man.

What made fatherhood so special to him was the fact that he and his wife had been convinced they would never have children. At first, not being able to have children had disturbed them, but after fifty years of marriage without being blessed with a child, they had come to accept that they would have no heirs.

But one day God spoke to the old man and told him that he would indeed be a father. He was so excited that he ran and told his wife. As any woman her age would have done, she just laughed and discounted the news.

The man wistfully remembered how he couldn't shake the idea that he was going to be a father. It hadn't been wishful thinking. He believed he would be a father because God told him it would happen. He had learned to trust God early and was convinced God would make him a father even though all the circumstances pointed away from that conclusion.

If Abraham's ultimate joy was his son Isaac, his greatest regret was the foolish mistake he made when he tried to help

God fulfill His promise. Abraham was so concerned that people would know God kept His word that he agreed to sleep with his wife's servant who was much younger. Sure enough, she had a baby, but it really wasn't much of a miracle. All it proved was that Sarah had been the one incapable of having children all those years. And what a mess it caused in the family. Abraham never really got over the sadness he felt on the day he had to send his firstborn and his son's mother away to keep peace in the family.

Abraham shook his head in astonishment as he thought about the events of the last thirty years. He thought about the lessons God had taught him, which he had been able to pass on to his sons. Probably the most dramatic lesson he had learned occurred on the day God told him to take his son up on a mountain to perform a sacrifice. What began as a simple act of worship turned into a huge lesson in faith and obedience that would shape his family's lives forever.

Abraham knew his days on earth were few. Like most fathers, he wondered what kind of impact he had really made on his son. He wondered if his son would pass on the truths he had shared with him. He wondered if his son's life would amount to anything after he was gone. He also wondered how God was going to make him the father of a great nation when his family was so small.

Although Abraham wondered about the future, he no longer doubted anything God had told him. He knew that if God said there would be a great nation coming from his lineage, it would happen. He knew he had transferred his faith to Isaac, and he was confident that somehow God would do what He had promised. How could he doubt? A quick glance toward the field was all Abraham needed to be assured of God's faithfulness.

Gaining Perspective

"Now faith is the assurance of things hoped for, the conviction of things not seen" (Hebrews 11:1). So opens the famous "Hall of Faith" chapter in the letter to the Hebrews. One of the prominent names mentioned in the chapter is Abraham.

Abraham's listing in Hebrews 11 is well deserved. From the first mention of Abraham in the Bible, God was challenging him to be a person of faith. God asked him to leave his comfortable lifestyle in Babylon and step out into the unknown. When Abraham entered a foreign land, God told him that his descendants would one day possess the land. And when he finally had a miracle son by Sarah, God tested his faith once again by challenging him to lay his son on the altar.

Each time Abraham took a leap of faith into the unknown, God was there to slip His divine hand under Abraham's suspended foot and set it on firm ground. Each time Abraham proved God, it reinforced the nature of God in his own life and in the lives of those who witnessed God's faithfulness through his life.

Abraham's reward for having faith in God was a great heritage. He didn't see all of God's promises fulfilled while he lived, but if he could have seen the way God used his children and grandchildren, he would have been pleased. Isaac, Jacob, and Joseph are names that will never be forgotten. Each built his faith on the foundation laid by Abraham. It was a legacy that would cause any father to be proud.

The difference between those who are mightily used by God and those who limp along in the Christian life is often determined by the individual's willingness to step out in faith. God will always ask us to do things that are uncomfortable for us. He does this to stretch us and to encourage us to depend on Him more fully. Those who accept this challenge walk a very exciting pathway in life. Those who choose to resist any new challenge learn to accept the mundane of safety and seldom make a mark on their culture.

As teachers, we have individuals in our classes who watch our lives and learn a great deal about God by the way we experience Him. We have the promise that our students and families will do even greater things than we have done (John 14:12). This is truly a legacy worth developing.

Observing the life of Abraham provides key principles that will help us as we prepare others to do greater works than we will ever accomplish. If we apply these principles to our teaching, we can look forward to the development of spiritual Isaacs, Jacobs, and Josephs as a result of our efforts.

Gleaning Principles

1. Don't Sugarcoat the Cost

As teachers, we hope to reproduce our better qualities in our students. We want our students to become people of faith. We want them to take spiritual risks as they follow God with abandon. But sometimes we try to hide the cost of faith because we don't want to scare them away.

The truth is that walking in faith can be uncomfortable. Telling our students that following Jesus is a cakewalk is a lie that will do more long-term damage than if we are up-front about the costs of faithful living. Many people have walked away from their faith when confronted with difficult situations because they were caught off guard. We do our students a favor by sharing with them the *costs* of faith as well as the *rewards*.

Some teachers make the mistake of telling their students that God's will for them will always be something they don't want to do. Some students wrongly believe that if they express a dislike for some type of work, God will call them to that work; or if they express a fear of going to a certain area of the world, God will be sure to send them there. God seldom does either. The truth is that God knows your students better than they even know themselves, and He will work with them to develop them in a way that will maximize their usefulness to Him. When this occurs, individuals experience a sense of purpose and fulfillment.

As one examines the choices Abraham had to make to please God, the great cost becomes readily apparent. Further examination demonstrates that God rewarded Abraham and provided much more fulfillment than he could have accomplished by his own design.

We must help our students understand that although living by faith has its challenges, the alternative is to accept less than all God desires for them.

2. Don't Hide Your Humanity

Abraham was a man of faith, but he blew it from time to time as well. No one will ever forget his choice to save his own life by making his wife available to a foreign king (Genesis 20:1–18). Although some would argue that he didn't technically lie, the truth is that he wasn't showing much faith in God at this particular moment in his life.

Abraham's lack of faith was very evident to all those around him, and the consequences of his lack of faith were public as well. Unfortunately, most of our choices that reflect a lack of faith are hidden. We fail to pay our tithes because we don't know how we are going to pay the utilities, and few people know. We refuse to talk to someone God instructs us to address because we are afraid, and the event goes by without notice. We feel God directing us to become involved in a new ministry, but we carry on in the comfort of the familiar, and no one expects anything different.

The reason our hidden lack of faith is unfortunate is twofold. First, when we make faithless decisions, consequences impact our lives that we often don't associate with the faithless act. If others saw the faithless act, they might have the opportunity to point out our error and the remedy. Financial troubles frequently are directly associated with our refusal to trust God enough with our finances to give Him the tithe He demands from His followers. Our lack of faith to address situations can lead to further troubles with persons or the situations themselves. And many times dissatisfaction with life is associated with a person's refusal to follow God into a new area of ministry. Living a faithless life is personally damaging.

The second reason a hidden lack of faith is unfortunate is that others cannot benefit from the lessons we learn if they do not know about them. Abraham's experience became a teaching opportunity for those who were with him. Granted, it took two experiences to learn the lesson concerning his fear of foreign leaders, but even this was a good lesson for his students. In the same way, if we will allow our students a glimpse into our failures and their consequences, we will provide our students with valuable lessons that will help them develop their own faith.

We would be foolish to think that we will never fail in our obedience to God. None of our students expects us to be perfect. When we are willing to be honest about our failures, we will enhance our ability to encourage our students to take a risk when God asks them to do so.

3. Reinforce the Potential

One of Abraham's greatest attributes was his ability to keep his eyes focused on the future. God promised him a son, a land, and a nation. Many things came into his life that could have distracted him from focusing on these promises. Even when he slipped up by becoming impatient and trying to take things into his own hands, he was able to work through his situation and make the necessary adjustments to get back on track.

A quality that teachers must seek to acquire is to be forward thinking. Teachers must keep the ultimate goal in mind as they go about their tasks. That goal is to develop students and help them become all they can be.

It is tempting to look at our students and judge which ones will make something out of themselves and which ones will do very little. Often we are guilty of treating our students according to this prejudice. There is no place for this type of judgment in the Sunday School classroom. Every student, without exception, has great potential in the kingdom of God. All of our students can be great in the Kingdom as they become the people God has designed them to be (see 1 Corinthians 12).

When we look at our students with eyes of potential, we see them with the eyes of God. Some of our students will be a challenge, but we are never given the right to write them off. As long as they are in our classrooms, we must see them as diamonds in the rough.

It is instructional to watch Abraham's interaction with Ishmael. He was not going to be the promised son who would fulfill God's promise, and his existence caused Abraham a great deal of heartache. But Abraham realized Ishmael could have a bright future. When Abraham sent Ishmael away with his mother, he did so knowing that God would take care of him. He believed God would accomplish His will in his son's life (Genesis 21:9–21).

Not only is it important for you to keep your students' potential in focus, but you must also help your students see their own potential. Students often bring a low self-esteem into the classroom. They have been told by parents, teachers, and coworkers that they are worthless. They need to hear that God believes in them and has a plan for them, and that they can do great things if they will become people of faith. When you do this, you are laying the foundation that is necessary to allow God to do what He desires to do in your students' lives.

4. Recognize the Power of an Example

Few biblical accounts show a more involved father than Abraham. Abraham definitely loved his sons and spent quality time with them. His hands-on approach to parenting produced sons who learned to trust God in very difficult times.

When Ishmael and his mother were sent from Abraham's home, Ishmael demonstrated faith in God even though it appeared he would die. Isaac repeatedly demonstrated faith in God throughout his life. One of the first examples of this is seen on the day he and his father went to the mountain to sacrifice (see Genesis 22:1–18).

The type of faith displayed by Ishmael and Isaac seldom comes without an example of how faith works. Because Abraham was a living example of faith, he didn't need to instruct his sons about faith in a formal way. Abraham's entire life was driven by his belief that one day his descendants would be as numerous as the sand. This wasn't a pipe dream; it was based on a clear promise from God that he knew he could trust (Genesis 17:16,17; 22:17,18).

Abraham's sons saw the way he lived and learned to embrace the God of their father. No one can shake the reality that God exists and can be trusted if they have been given a strong example by someone they respect. Even if they run from the truth, they will never be able to get away from it.

As teachers, we must remember the power of example. If you

teach children and they have parents who demonstrate faith in God, it is important for you to reinforce this faith to their child by including the parents in classroom activities when possible. Cite examples from the parents' lives in your lessons and encourage your students to follow their parents' example.

If you teach adults or have students who do not come from strong Christian homes, you may have to step in and be an example of faith for your students. This should simply be a natural extension of your everyday life. Your students will quickly determine what drives your life, and many will embrace that zeal for their own lives. If they see that your life revolves around football, many will learn to love football. If it revolves around fishing, many will learn to fish. If it revolves around your love of Jesus, many will learn to love Jesus.

Some of your more difficult students will be those who come from homes and backgrounds without an active faith in God. They may be either churched or unchurched. The best way to perpetuate truth to these individuals is through consistently living out your faith in front of them week after week. As you gain their trust and respect, they will embrace your faith and your Father.

Giving It a Try

1. Being Honest About the Cost

Often when we teach, we are afraid to share the tough side of living for Christ because we think it will scare people away. However, often the very reason people walk away from the gospel is this lack of preparation for facing opposition in the real world. People who know that their faith comes with a cost and accept that up front are much more likely to remain standing when the storms come their way.

Most people want to make a difference in this world and

want to embrace a worthy cause. They are willing to make a personal sacrifice if that sacrifice will lead to a meaningful result. Help students to see that there is nothing more significant than to perpetuate the truth of God's Word from generation to generation and that they can be active participants in this process.

Don't dwell on the challenges of living for Christ, but regularly provide examples of biblical characters as well as contemporary characters who faced opposition to their faith. Be sure to help students see God's faithfulness to these individuals in their times of trouble even when things didn't turn out as one might desire. Not all of the biblical examples of opposition turn out as neatly as Daniel's experience in the lions' den or the Hebrew children's success in the furnace. Stephen, James, and Jesus each were required to pay the ultimate price for their obedience to God. Help students see that what happens to them is not as important as what God is able to do through them as they faithfully serve Him.

2. Being Honest About Your Humanity

People who attend our Sunday School classes often look up to us. Most believe that we teachers are spiritual people, and some of our authority is derived from this belief. It is risky to let people see inside our lives and realize that we blow it from time to time. Because of that risk, sometimes we attempt to cover our mistakes and hide them from those we teach.

A bigger risk is associated with cover-up than with humble exposure. In recent years, many U.S. political leaders have tried to cover their mistakes only to make matters worse. Watergate, "Iran gate," "Monica gate," and a variety of other "gates" could have turned out so much better if these presidents had come clean early in the process and simply confessed their sin and sought redemption.

If Abraham could blow it, how can we think *we* are exempt from the possibility of acting in a faithless manner? We must be quick to reveal our faults before those who have placed their spiritual trust in us, and quick to demonstrate true repentance. Providing graphic details of our missteps is not necessary, but we need to let our students know how to regain their spiritual position when they have made decisions that have disappointed God.

3. Reinforcing the Potential

You may not be aware of how much power you hold over your students' lives. Many people have shaped their lives according to the words of their teachers. Some have limited their lives by the restraints teachers have put on them through words of discouragement. Others have gone beyond their natural abilities as a result of an encouraging teacher. Perhaps your life has been shaped by a teacher from your past.

Finding ways to identify areas of your students' lives that could be maximized is vital. Perhaps a student speaks well, has an ability to work with his or her hands, has musical or artistic abilities, or is skilled in the use of the language. When you identify a skill, be sure to tell the student what you see, and give him or her praise and encouragement to develop the skill as a ministry to God. Your words of encouragement are powerful, but sadly, they may be the only words of encouragement your students receive.

At times you may need to direct students away from an area because they think they have skills that in reality they do not have. Before you discourage them, help them explore ways to enhance the talent they seek to use. When that route is exhausted, you will do the student a favor by gently offering guidance that will help him or her avoid expending time and effort in an area of futility. Gentleness is key when employing this type of guidance, and it can only be done effectively if a good relationship has been established in advance.

In addition to personal encouragement, you can cultivate potential by placing motivational posters on your classroom walls, using positive can-do examples in your lessons, and bringing guest teachers into your classroom who have positive testimonies of what God did in their lives to cultivate their potential. This type of motivation is not limited to children and youth; adults also need to be challenged to develop their potential and can do great things for God even in their older years.

4. Being an Example

Like it or not, you are an example for your students. Your likes will often translate into the likes of your students. If you use the New King James Version, most of your students will use that translation. If you are excited about learning, your students will come to class excited. If you are involved in community work and talk about it, some in your class will follow in your footsteps.

You must be careful that your example remains positive. Be careful not to criticize leaders even if they are political leaders in some faraway city. When you criticize a leader, you are granting permission to your students to criticize their leaders, including their pastors, parents, and you. Likewise, we must set good examples in the areas of attitude, respect for God's Word, church attendance, service, and faithfulness.

Abraham transmitted his faith to his household because they saw how central it was to his life. We also have the opportunity to transfer our faith if it is truly valuable to us.

It Works

The Sylvester and Skinner farm is a place that holds many positive memories for me. As a teen, I spent many long, hot summer days there picking peas and strawberries. As I grew a little older, I began to do other jobs on the farm. I would hoe strawberry rows, plow fields, supervise field workers, and drive the crops to market.

More significant for me than the money I earned and the experience I gained in the fields was the time I got to spend talking with and observing the owner of the farm. He was a special man in my life. Not only was he my employer, but he was also my Sunday School teacher.

Bert Skinner understood that the spiritual development of a young man could not be limited to the classroom. There was no doubt that the lessons he taught each Sunday made an impact on me, but the time and energy he invested in me outside the classroom made the biblical truths he taught come alive.

Bert's investment in me came at a cost to him and his family. At times they would have been better off financially to let me go. Bert resisted making the wise fiscal decision. He understood that the long-term results of the time he was able to invest in me would justify the monetary investment.

Some of the most memorable times for me were the trips home from the farm. I was too young to drive, so my parents would drop me off, and Bert would drive me home. All along the way, Bert would talk to me about God, about my life, and about the world at-large. He would pull his truck into the driveway of my home, and we would sit sometimes for an hour and just talk. He would tell me things from his past, give testimony of God's goodness, and provide fatherly advice. I remember loving the attention and hearing his stories. Even as a teenager, I saw how costly Bert's investment in me was and appreciated it.

As a personal friend of Bert's sons, I had the opportunity to see him in many contexts. Bert wasn't perfect, but he was authentic. He lived his life the same no matter where he was or what he was doing. He was a gentle man with a quick wit and a great sense of humor, but he was always ready to exhort those who needed it. When he made a mistake, he didn't try to hide it. His humility was something nearly all who knew him appreciated. It wasn't long before Bert's God became my God in a more powerful way. There was no question that he was in love with God and that living for God was his highest priority.

Bert saw my potential as well as my limitations. I will never forget the day I sat at his table and he looked across at me and said, "You need to find a job where you can use your head, because you don't have any ability to use your hands." I didn't take offense at what Bert said that day, because he had earned the right to speak into my life. His words propelled a kid to begin thinking about college. Without his sage advice, I may never have found a path that led to my satisfaction and success.

Bert Skinner was just one of my Sunday School teachers, but his example outside the classroom made him the most effective teacher I have ever had. Like Abraham, he lived his faith every day for all to see. He never showed any pretense or a desire to have people look at him. He didn't like attention, but attention always seemed to find him, because that kind of faith isn't easily ignored. I am thankful for Bert Skinner's influence and his willingness to pass his faith on to me.

The Rest of the Story

If Abraham could sit beside you today and have you tell him about the history of the Middle East, he would be amazed but not surprised. Although he only personally saw eight sons born to him (see Genesis 16:15; 21:2; 25:1), he knew that someday he would have many more descendants. He probably would be amazed at *how* God pulled it off, but not by the fact that He *did*.

Abraham would be sad at the conflict his misstep brought to the world. He might even wonder how things would have turned out if he would have had a little more faith that God could give him a child without Abraham's manipulation of circumstances.

Abraham would be a little embarrassed by all the attention he has received throughout the years. And he probably would be a little self-conscious about being labeled as the father of the faith. In his mind's eye, he wasn't all that faithful. He really hadn't done anything that anyone else wouldn't have done if God had come to the door and given similar instructions.

Amazed, sad, embarrassed, yes, but Abraham's greatest emotion would be pleasure. He would be pleased that his life had made a difference. He would be pleased that the faith that he had in his God was passed down from generation to generation. He would be pleased because his children, grandchildren, and great-grandchildren made it possible for there to be a Messiah to deliver salvation to the world. He would be pleased that his family circle had become wide enough to include those who were not a natural part of his family tree. He would be pleased that he had decided to say yes on that fateful day when God had approached him at his home in Ur.

Conclusion

You may not feel that your teaching is having a great impact, but don't let those feelings dissuade you from doing the work God has called you to do. Abraham never saw the evidence that his life would have such long-term influence. He had to believe that God was telling him the truth when He shared concerning his life's potential.

God has told us that our ministries will have a similar outcome. We can believe that if we are faithful in our calling, live an authentic life before our students, and encourage the potential in our students, many generations to come will be blessed.

Personal Reflection

1. What is your teaching ministry costing you personally in time, energy, and finances?
2. Why do you think it is difficult to admit your human frailties?
3. What can you do to become better at identifying and encouraging potential in your students?
4. Whose example has made the biggest impact on your life and why?

CHAPTER 3

Perpetuating Truth Through **Compassion**

*Kindness has converted
more sinners than zeal,
eloquence, or learning.*

~ Frederick W. Faber

Sweat rolled down the middle-aged man's face as he sat in the hot, sun-drenched field watching his sheep. His mind once again wandered back to the days of his youth, which seemed so distant now. Those had been confusing days. He had been torn between the life of luxury that surrounded him and a vision that would force him to abandon what could only be hoped for by so many in his community.

He easily could have thought that all of his sacrifices had gone unrewarded. He had traded the possibility of ruling an entire nation for what would be considered by many a pipe dream. But he couldn't shake the lessons he had learned on the knee of his nurse. She had whispered in his ear that God loved him. She had told him that God had a plan for his life and that he had been selected to do a special work for God and for those who were enslaved by his father. He had been taught that God loved everyone and that he should respect all people regardless of their heritage. This woman seemed like a mother to him. He felt a bond as she nourished his heart as well as his body.

He wished that he could put his finger on what had come over him that fateful day. He had seen many of the slaves beaten and treated unfairly. It seemed like the supervisors did everything they could to provoke the slaves. But on this day, he reached his limit. He really hadn't meant for it to go this far, but he lost control. He was enraged, not by hatred for the man he killed, but by the love that he felt for the powerless one who was suffering such cruelty. He was driven to act as a defender. How silly he felt when the very people he tried to defend later ridiculed him and turned their back on him. But it didn't really matter, because inside he knew his motives were a reflection of what he believed.

His steamy perspiration turned into a cold sweat as he thought about the day Pharaoh tried to have him killed. He barely made it out of the courtyard alive. How he reached the land of Midian was still a mystery to him. But in some way, he was convinced that his escape was a gift from the Hebrew God in whom he believed.

He laughed as he recalled his first encounter in Midian. He had thought he was hallucinating, but as he drew closer to the well, he knew what he was seeing was real. To his delight, there stood seven beautiful women drawing water for their father's sheep.

Just as he started to strike up a conversation with the women, some shepherds approached and tried to run them off. The same righteous anger that caused him to kill the Egyptian arose in his heart toward these shepherds. He couldn't help himself. He couldn't allow the weak to suffer at the hands of the mighty. He had to defend these women, so he drove the shepherds away. The reward for his actions was much better this time: he was given one of the daughters to be his wife.

His flashback was interrupted by the crackling sound of fire. He turned and saw a burning bush. He stood and watched it. He was puzzled because the bush continued to burn but did not turn to ash. Then his puzzlement turned to shock as a voice called out his name from the midst of the fire. To say the least, the situation had caught his attention. In the next few minutes Moses would learn his destiny.

Gaining Perspective

Moses' act of defending the Hebrew slave would have been considered brave by some but unwise by most others in his day. Why would he risk everything he had to help someone who had no power to help him? Even after doing such a noble thing, he was ridiculed by the very people to whom he reached out.

We may not live in the Egyptian kingdom of the biblical era, but many of the philosophies that drove the leaders of that kingdom are still present in our world today. From our earliest days, society teaches us that the powerful are to be revered and the powerless are to be exploited. If individuals possess the commodities valued by society, such as beauty, wealth, strength, and intelligence, they will likely feel accepted in any crowd. If they lack these qualities, they will accept inferior treatment, believing they deserve nothing more.

Look around any elementary school and you will see these principles at work. The strong young boys rule the playground while the pretty little girls gain the attention of the teachers and their fellow students. The principles don't change in junior high or high school when crucial self-esteem issues shape the welfare of young men and women for many years to come. We would be kidding ourselves to believe that we grow beyond these principles when we become adults. You probably could make a list of the "haves" and the "have-nots" in your workplace and clearly know where you fit.

Reaching out to those who are in a lower class than your own is risky. Few want to take a chance that they will be contaminated by an association with those who are less fortunate. Because they are fearful of retribution by others, many turn their heads when the less fortunate are treated unfairly. As a result, a gulf continually exists between the "acceptable" group and the "unacceptable," with very few bridges available to link the two.

Unfortunately, many of society's philosophies have found their way into the Church. Although antithetical to the teachings of Jesus, cliques can be identified easily in most churches. The criteria for becoming a part of the spiritual "in-crowd" is much the same as that used for endorsing people in other settings. We tend to reward those who have talent, money, intelligence, or a pleasant appearance.

Our tendency to embrace the world's philosophy of exclusiveness is seen not only in the way we treat people in the church, but also is reflected in our attitude toward those who need to know Jesus outside of the church. Many are afraid their reputation will be soiled if they associate with sinners. They would rather go about their comfortable lives ignoring the eternal plight of these people. Jesus provides a clear example of this type of attitude in His parable of the good Samaritan (Luke 10:30–37).

When Moses stood against the philosophy of his society by defending the disenfranchised, he didn't do it in his own strength. He was compelled by compassion and driven by a desire to see justice for all regardless of their station in life.

Within a very short time, Moses' decision cost him everything. But eventually his decision resulted in an entire nation being set free from bondage, and in God's truth being perpetuated throughout the generations.

As Christian teachers, we are confronted with the same difficult choice Moses had. We can go about our comfortable "business as usual" approach, ministering exclusively to our own "kind," or we can take it upon ourselves to reach out to those beyond our circle who need our assistance. Following Moses' lead is risky business, but the reward for doing so will be the opportunity to see people set free from bondage and begin a new spiritual legacy that will affect many generations to come.

Gleaning Principles

1. We Must Understand Our Mission

Have you ever asked yourself why you are a teacher? What is your purpose and goal for your class? What do you want to get out of the experience?

Determining if you are primarily a teacher-focused teacher or a student-focused teacher is vital. Teacher-focused teachers are more concerned about their ability to communicate a message than they are about the student's ability to learn the lesson. Many teacher-focused teachers enjoy the praise they receive for their talent, knowledge, and willingness to be used by God. Their experience is very rewarding as long as the students cooperate.

Student-focused teachers have the welfare of their students as a primary goal. How long it takes to get through to a student isn't an issue as long as the student grasps the concepts being learned. These teachers don't always have the quietest classrooms or the most desirable students, but this isn't of greatest concern to them. They understand that their mission is to help those who need help the most and to do whatever it takes to help their students more fully develop their relationship with God.

The mission Jesus gave us was student focused (Matthew 28:19,20). He instructed us to go outside of our comfort zones and set the captives free. He never called us to be great performers or to teach for our own benefit. Teaching done correctly is a sacrifice and service. Our ultimate mission is to invest in individuals who will one day invest in others. If each generation of teachers accomplishes this mission, the truth of God will continue to be perpetuated throughout time.

2. We Must See People the Way God Sees Them

Moses didn't fully understand his mission when he first intervened in the affairs of the Hebrew slaves, but he couldn't just sit by and let the abuse continue. Those being abused were not necessarily Moses' friends or even acquaintances, but they were people, and that was enough. They didn't deserve to be mistreated.

We can easily become so focused on our own lives that we don't take the time to look around us and see the suffering in our world. Like the multitude of Egyptians who walked by without intervening in the suffering of the Hebrews, we can be guilty of walking past the masses without identifying with their struggles.

As Christian teachers, we can't afford to be spiritually myopic. We must see all of humanity with the eyes of God. We must be touched by the feelings of the student who is left out of a game or a conversation. We must have compassion for the AIDS patient and for the teen mother who walks through the doorway of an abortion center. We must identify with the homeless, the jobless, and those who seem to make all the wrong choices. We must not become like them, but we must see them as people God wants to bless through us and through the lives of our students.

It is nearly impossible to see the needs of hurting people without being among them. Certainly there are plenty of hurts represented in our sanitized sanctuaries and Sunday School classrooms, and we must minister to these needs. But there are so many more people that could be reached if we were willing to get out among the hurting and view them with eyes of compassion. When we do this, we reflect the ministry and priorities of Jesus, who spent a great deal of His time ministering to those no "self-respecting" Jew would address. Jesus willingly ministered to the disenfranchised of His world. As Christians we must follow His example (Matthew 25:34–40).

3. We Must Be Willing to Take a Risk

Moses took a major risk when he rescued the Hebrew slave. The moment he made the decision to intervene in the Jewish situation, he knew life would be different. But he felt the risk was worth taking because he believed the unfair treatment of the slaves had to end.

Those in the business world understand that you will seldom get a big return unless a big risk is involved. Those who are content in keeping what they have will seldom get more. Jesus told the Parable of the Talents to illustrate the importance of "risk taking" within His kingdom (Matthew 25:14–30).

Taking risks generally means trying things you haven't tried before. Perhaps it will mean trying a new method in your classroom. Perhaps it will mean spending time with your students outside of class or being willing to get involved in their personal lives and problems. Perhaps it will mean getting involved personally in an outreach to the disenfranchised in your community and then getting your class involved.

God encourages us to take a risk, because when we do so we are forced into "faith" situations. Only when we take a step outside our comfort zone can we truly learn to trust God. Perhaps you remember the feeling of inadequacy you had when you taught for the first time. That feeling of inadequacy forced you to trust God and grow in Him. Taking a risk will place you back into a growth mode as God stretches you and shapes you into the person He desires.

Before we will be willing to take a risk, we must feel that the results will warrant the potential sacrifice. Moses decided that freedom from oppression was a worthy cause. We must decide if we are willing to make a similar bold move in order to see spiritual captives set free from the oppression imposed on them by the enemy of their souls.

4. We Must Be Willing to Live With the Consequences

Things didn't turn out for Moses the way he anticipated. Instead of cheers from the grateful Hebrew slaves, he got jeers (Exodus 2:13,14). His brave move cost him every creature comfort he had accumulated to that point in his life. Everything seemed to vanish before his eyes as a result of doing something he felt was right.

We have no guarantee that doing the right thing will result in immediate rewards. Sometimes the opposite occurs because our actions are misunderstood or misinterpreted. Sometimes our righteous actions cause others to feel guilty, and the only way they know how to deal with the guilt is to try to get us to stop doing righteous actions. Others will reject our righteous actions simply because of their own carnality or fear of losing what they have. This was the case with the Pharisees who sought to destroy Jesus for His righteous actions (Matthew 23:1–12).

We must be willing to do what is right regardless of the consequences. The life of righteousness we model for our students will not always be accepted, but it will be noticed and will make an impact on their lives. In the end, it really doesn't matter how people react to our choices as long as our choices please God.

If you reach out to the disenfranchised in your community, you will likely face some resistance from people in your church. In the short run, your reputation may be questioned and you may even lose some of your influence. But in the long run, you will be blessed by the smile of your Father and by the multitude of individuals who were once bound but have now been set free. Those are consequences that most teachers would be willing to endure.

Giving It a Try

1. Making a Choice to Be Student Focused

Fully understanding our mission as being student focused will change the way we approach our class. Instead of spending all of our time getting a lesson ready, we will invest more time in developing our students throughout the week through prayer, personal interaction, and preparing ourselves to relate more effectively to them. Obviously we must prepare to teach each week, but our emphasis will be on communicating with the students rather than simply communicating a message.

How can you tell if you are a student-focused teacher? One of the clearest ways is by listening to your own postsession questions. If you ask, "How did I do today?" you are probably primarily a teacher-focused teacher. If you ask, "Did I get through the material today?" you are probably primarily a subject-focused teacher. If you ask, "What did the students learn today?" you are probably a student-focused teacher.

Student-focused teachers will always answer the "So what?" question. Providing solid biblical information is not enough. That is the starting point, but your students want to know, "So what does it have to do with me?" This is especially true the older the students you teach. Teens and adults increasingly become problem centered in their learning rather than subject centered. For example, they don't really care who the judges were in the Old Testament unless you can help them identify the transcultural principles that will impact their lives in a positive manner.

Student-focused teachers will demand that students participate in the learning process. This is commonly done in the younger age groups through hands-on learning and guided play. The older groups often accomplish this through discussion and service projects. One of the most difficult transitions teachers make from being teacher focused to becoming student focused is to transfer the responsibility of discovering truth to their students. Student-focused teachers do not see their primary task as transferring information they have learned to their students. These teachers insist that their students grapple with the implications of the biblical text using age-appropriate methods to personally arrive at conclusions. They understand that we learn best when we actively participate in the learning process.

Student-focused teachers care more about the spiritual development of students than the presentation of biblical facts. This trait is revealed by observing what gets emphasized in the lesson. Many teachers find themselves running out of time talking about the content of the lesson while leaving the lesson application unexplored. These teachers dismiss the class all too often with the statement, "Sorry we didn't finish the lesson, but we will get back to it next week." Seldom do they revisit the lesson, and a perfectly good biblical principle lies dormant unless some exceptional student happens to pick it up.

Student-focused teachers refuse to leave application to chance. They weave application throughout the class period and challenge students to do something with what they have heard. They will at minimum challenge the students to live the life they have learned about and provide a few concrete examples of how to do it.

2. Seeing People With God's Eyes

The first step in seeing people with God's eyes is to see yourself with God's eyes. Often our skewed view of self leads us to be exceedingly judgmental of others. It is impossible to love people properly if you have not learned to love yourself in a healthy manner (Matthew 7:12).

The Bible tells us to think about ourselves properly (Galatians 6:3). We are not to view ourselves either too highly or too lowly. God loves us supremely but no more than any other person He created. You are extremely special but no more special than anyone else. You are accepted by God regardless of your sin, and so is everyone else.

Once we see ourselves properly, our focus can be outward rather than inward. We can look around and see the needs of individuals and have compassion for them. We begin to identify with their situations and reach out to them rather than judge them, because we realize that they are no different than we are except for the grace of God.

This transformation seldom happens in isolation. Sitting in judgment of a person is easier if you are not near to that person. Criticizing the decisions of a young woman who has an abortion is easy until that young girl is your own daughter. Criticizing those who divorce is easy until your son is the one getting the divorce. Looking down on the homeless is easy until you are faced with losing your own home.

If you truly want to see people with God's eyes, you need to step out of your comfort zone and spend some time with the people in greatest need. This is the approach Jesus took when He came to live among us and to learn more personally what we experience (Hebrews 2:18).

Sharing your new insights with your students as you are developing the eyes of God is important. Some individuals in your class will be prejudiced and bigoted. They may not appreciate your acceptance of sinners as equals in God's sight. They may have so embraced the world's standards that they believe only the strong, smart, and solvent should be valued. Help them to see that God loves the outcast and to embrace God's view of humanity.

3. Taking a Risk

Moses took a risk by reaching out to help a defenseless person, an act totally out of character for a person in his position. He was a member of the elite, and to defend such lowly people was unheard of. But Moses couldn't help himself when he saw what was happening.

As Christians who see people the way God sees them, we will be compelled to do something about their situation. We will have to reach out to the "lowlifes" and offer them the same gift of salvation we have been given. We will be compelled to invite sinners to our sanctuaries and classrooms. We will not be able to refrain from sharing with our students the burden of reaching the lost. We will design class projects that reach out to those who are in need. We will do the things God has called us to do (James 1:27).

Obeying God's commands should not come with a risk of rejection by those in the body of Christ, but it does. Some people are more concerned about the cleanliness of a building than about the cleanliness of a person's soul. Some will criticize your outreach efforts. And some will simply ignore your efforts and make believe you aren't there.

The risk isn't only with those in the church. Reaching out to the disenfranchised can be costly and can result in your being manipulated. Your efforts may result in a drunk being able to buy more wine or a con artist walking away with your hard-earned money. Worse, the people you reach out to may accept your help but reject your God much like what happened in Moses' case.

Not all risks do produce positive results, yet if we don't take risks, we will not likely see many people released from the bonds that hold them. Ultimately, the reason we must take risks is because this is our mandate from God. He has told us to go out and spread the gospel beyond our comfort zone. This task is so vital that He has provided special power to help us accomplish it (Acts 1:8).

At some point in each of our spiritual family trees, someone took a risk to reach out to us. We have a responsibility to return the favor by making a spiritual investment in others who need to be set free to live in the freedom of Christ.

4. Living With the Consequences

Jesus loved us so much that He willingly gave His life for us even when it wasn't appreciated (John 1:11). Are you willing to step out in faith without knowing what the results will be?

Some may think of this statement as reckless. And in a way it is. Living the Christian faith the way Jesus taught it is reckless. He told the rich man to go and sell all he had and then follow Him (Luke 18:18–34). This seemed too reckless to the man, and he refused to follow Jesus. Andrew and Peter, on the other hand, walked away from their nets to spend an unspecified time with Jesus. Their names will be remembered forever because of their reckless act.

Have you ever wondered what we would have known about Moses if he had not acted in a reckless fashion? He may have lived a comfortable life, but it would not have amounted to much in historical terms. But his reckless act led to the Exodus, the formation of a nation, and to your salvation.

Moses did have to wait a considerable amount of time before his reckless act turned into anything positive. And he probably had no clue until the burning bush that his act had been so significant. But desire for fame did not propel him to help the slaves. He helped them because they needed help and he had the power to do something.

As Christians, we have the power to help those who need help. When we reach out to the lost, we may not see immediate results. We must remember the lesson of Moses and realize that the results may come later. We must also realize that the results are God's responsibility.

We have no guarantee of positive spiritual results when we reach out to people, but there is a guaranteed result if they never hear the gospel. If people do not hear about Jesus, they will remain in bondage and ultimately spend eternity in hell. In order for us to perpetuate the truth, we must be willing to take a risk and live with the consequences. Only the future will reveal the results of such a bold move.

It Works

Three young boys and a girl tragically lost their father in an automobile accident. The kids' dad was a preacher and had not been able to plan financially for his untimely death. Their mother struggled to make ends meet. Fortunately, people in the church and the community reached out to the family in compassion and love.

As the boys grew, they committed themselves to do for others what others had done for them. They vowed that if they ever had a chance to make a difference in the lives of hurting people, they would do so.

One of the young men decided that he needed to get to know more about the plight of the poor. He wanted to see them through the eyes of God and knew that the only way he could do so would be to spend some time with them. He decided to go to a number of major U.S. cities and interview the homeless, gang members, prostitutes, runaways, and others. His experiences opened his eyes wider than he ever expected.

Out of his desire to help, this young man and his brothers started a ministry called Convoy of Hope, an organization designed to provide, in a dignified manner, physical and spiritual food to those in need. Guests come to the Convoy of Hope ministry site in local communities as a result of advertisement or invitation. They receive bags of groceries, haircuts, health care, and a variety of other services they may not get other places. The children are treated to games and goodies. The entire day's events are filled with fun and joy for both the recipients and the givers.

Hal Donaldson took a risk when he went to stay on the city streets. He and his brothers took a risk to launch a ministry they weren't sure others would support. In the early years, they took a risk by scheduling events without really knowing if anyone would show up to take advantage of what they were providing. And they also took a risk that perhaps people would come for the physical food but reject the spiritual food they so desperately wanted to provide.

Convoy of Hope has made a major impact around the world. Hundreds of thousands of people visit a Convoy site each year. Major donors have seen Convoy's value and have provided tons of food, financial assistance, and trucks to move the goods from place to place. But most important, thousands of people have heard the gospel, and many have responded to the good news. Families have been transformed, hope has been given, and God's truth has been perpetuated because three young men began to see people with the eyes of God and did something about it.

The Rest of the Story

Moses walked away from the burning bush challenged. Why had God chosen him to lead the Hebrews out of Egypt? And what was the staff thing all about? He didn't know how he was going to pull it off, but how could he say no to God?

Moses' life was a series of risks from that time forward. Each time he did what he was told, God came through for him. The only time Moses had real trouble was when he tried to do things in his own strength. How he wished he hadn't struck that rock when God told him to speak to it.

As Moses grew old, he often reflected on his life. Early on, he reached out and helped someone in distress, and as a reward, God had given him thousands of followers who were committed to serving God. Yes, it would have been easier if the spies had come back with a faithful report forty years earlier, but it hadn't been all bad. Each day Moses had learned to trust God for all of their supplies. Now he would trust God with his own spiritual destiny and with the destiny of a nation. Moses could shut his eyes and say with confidence that he had done his part in passing on God's truth to the next generation.

Conclusion

Moses' life was filled with adventure. He had the opportunity to lead a great nation. He personally encountered God and received the Ten Commandments and instructions for making the tabernacle. He also oversaw the formation of the priesthood for Israel. But all of these things would not have been possible if he had not had compassion for people early on in life and taken the risk to assist those who needed help.

Your greatest task as a teacher is to perpetuate truth to the next generation. You do this by sharing God's love with those who need it and then by helping them develop in Christ. As you do so, you are in the process of reproducing yourself for generations to come.

Are you willing to take the risks necessary to see even greater results from your ministry efforts? If you will step out in faith, God will be there to catch your foot and provide you a place to walk on in Him.

Personal Reflection

1. What steps can you take to become more student centered in your approach to teaching?
2. What steps could you take to see people more clearly as God sees them?
3. What outreach activity could you and your students become involved in this year?
4. What prevents you from living a reckless life in obedience to God?

CHAPTER 4

Perpetuating Truth Through **Leadership**

A great leader never sets himself above his followers except in carrying responsibilities.
~ Jules Ormont

The lonely man sat silently reflecting on the life and ministry of his mentor and friend. How he wished he could have been there when this great example of godliness drew his last breath. It would have been fitting considering the time they had spent together over the last forty years, but it wasn't to be. His friend wandered into the mountains like he had so many times before, but this time he didn't return. It was probably better that way. He didn't know how he would have handled seeing his friend dead.

Today was especially hard. If ever there was a time he needed advice, it was now. His friend had done a good job of preparing the man for the technicalities of the job he now held, but he never anticipated that being in charge could be so taxing on one's mind and spirit. He was learning that leadership takes every ounce of strength and wisdom a person possesses, especially when following in the footsteps of a great person who has provided leadership to a group of people for a long time. Even though this was a job he never really expected to have, he was glad for the opportunity to carry on the good work started by his predecessor.

His resolve was tested within days of the time he assumed the leadership role. The group had talked for a long time about making their dream move to another location, and God seemed to be saying that now was the time to make the move.

He shook his head as he thought about the irony. His friend had wanted to be the one to lead the people into this next phase of their journey, but he was not allowed to do so. Here he sat, a raw rookie as a leader, and he was being given the privilege and responsibility of making the move. It almost seemed unfair.

His task wasn't going to be easy, for he faced obstacles that seemed insurmountable. But he remembered how his mentor had faced a similar situation and had bravely called on God to give him guidance and strength to lead the people.

He was amazed at how well the move went, and after that first success as a leader, he became more confident. He wisely called on God and asked for his next assignment. The goal was large and the strategy seemed foolish, but who was he to question God? He had learned his lesson about questioning God's ability many years ago and wasn't going to let the people he led make that mistake again. Joshua was tired of sand, quail, and manna. He kind of liked the taste of milk and honey.

Everything seemed to be going well until just a few days ago. There was no way his army should have been defeated by the small army from the town of Ai. And now he found out the reason was because there was sin in the camp. What kind of leader was he that he would let this type of greed and disobedience spawn? He wished he had paid a little more attention when Moses had faced sin in the camp on the day he returned with God's commandments.

Joshua pondered his own effectiveness as a leader. He wondered if he would be able to pass the leadership of the nation on to his successor in as good shape as Moses had passed it to him.

Gaining Perspective

Can you imagine what it felt like for Joshua to stand before the nation of Israel for the first time after the report of Moses' death? Multiplied thousands of people who had daily looked to Moses for leadership over the last forty years now fixed their eyes on Joshua, wondering how life would be different under his leadership. If you have ever followed in the footsteps of a great leader, you may be able to relate to Joshua's situation.

Joshua had a few options. He could have run away from the responsibility and left the nation to fend for itself. He could have tried to be a clone of Moses since the people had liked him so much. Or he could have attempted to establish his own leadership style by relying on God to give him direction and guidance. Fortunately for the nation of Israel, Joshua chose the third option. His leadership was not a great deal like that of Moses. God was asking him to take the nation to a new place (Joshua 1:1–5).

It is tempting to try to model yourself after a great leader and to shape your teaching according to his or her style. Although there is merit in learning from the example of a great teacher, trying to mimic someone else's ministry in an attempt to duplicate it is never wise. God calls each of us to a unique ministry for a unique time in history. He wants each of us to lead our students to a new place as He leads us to a new place in our lives.

Joshua's job was not easy, and neither is yours. God continually reassured Joshua that He would be with him in his task. He also told him to be strong and courageous. These statements must have been comforting and disturbing at the same time. What in Joshua's future would require strength and courage? God's promise of companionship would have to be enough to sustain him.

God has promised to be with us as well in the task to which He has called us (Hebrews 13:5). We will experience obstacles to our work. Since perpetuating truth is the most important job Christians are called to accomplish in life, we can be sure that our spiritual enemy and his ambassadors will attempt to inhibit us from reaching our goal. In those trying times, being keenly aware of God's presence will allow us to be strong and courageous.

A quick examination of some of the techniques Joshua used to lead his people will reveal a few secrets that will help you to reach your goal of moving your students toward their promised land.

Gleaning Principles

1. Rely on God for Direction

Joshua was not only replacing a popular and successful leader, he was also being called to lead people on a new adventure into unknown territory. This type of responsibility could not be taken lightly. God had promised him success if he stayed on course. Joshua understood that he had to obey God and rely on Him to have any chance for success.

Note that although God gave Joshua an overview of what was going to happen during his leadership, He didn't tell Joshua the whole plan. Instead, God gave him one task at a time and specific instructions to follow to accomplish that task.

The way God worked with Joshua is often the way He works with leaders today, and that can be frustrating for those who want to have everything in focus for a few years down the road. If we can be satisfied with short-term directives from God, we will have no problem following Him and relishing the victories He provides. Only when we demand to have greater control of the work do we become dissatisfied leading God's people. Joshua's story demonstrates the wisdom of trusting God with the "big picture" of our lives and ministries while faithfully executing the short-term goals and tasks He places before us.

As teachers, we must live "in the moment" as we minister to our students. If we look too far ahead, we can become overwhelmed with the task. God has promised to provide the strength we need to accomplish the tasks He sets before us (2 Corinthians 12:9). We can be confident that when we need more strength, He will provide it. The key to victory is to not get in front of God. Like Joshua, we are required to keep God in our sights and go where He leads rather than where we might want to go (Joshua 3:1–4). When we do this, His desires will be accomplished and we will achieve our purpose.

2. Recount the Historical Facts

God instructed Joshua to build altars of remembrance at places where great miracles had taken place (e.g., Joshua 4:1–24). These altars of stone would serve as teaching points for the generations to come. God knew that in the future, each time parents and their children walked by one of these altars, it would provide the parent an opportunity to retell the story of God's faithfulness. Thus the children would learn about their godly heritage and be provided with an opportunity to talk about the magnitude of God, and parents would continually be able to draw strength from the past to help them face the difficulties of the present. God helped Joshua understand that the faith of future generations was built on the facts of history.

History has acquired a bad name in many segments of our society. We are so caught up in the busyness of today and tomorrow that we often ignore the lessons of the past. As

Sunday School teachers, we spend a great deal of time talking about biblical history, but how many of us draw illustrations and examples from the history of our denomination or local church? Quite possibly many teachers don't know the history of the church to which they belong. If this is the case, we rob our students of a great heritage designed to provide strength and hope to them.

We must remember that we didn't get to today without the assistance of yesterday. Our students, like the students of Joshua, should be made aware of the journey their forefathers took and the miracles God performed in their lives. These faith facts will provide a bridge of spiritual continuity from generation to generation.

3. Demand Accountability

Joshua faced a situation that no leader likes to encounter. One of his students willfully disregarded the mandates of God and was living in sin. At first Joshua didn't know who had committed the sin, but he was keenly aware of the impact this unknown sin was having on the entire nation of Israel.

Joshua's leadership was at a crossroads, and he was forced to make a choice. He could ignore the sin, avoid personal conflict, and allow the nation to suffer, or he could investigate the situation, confront the sinner, and free the nation to continue to receive God's blessings. Fortunately for the nation, he chose to confront the sin and the sinner, and rooted the sin out of the camp (Joshua 7:1–26).

On the surface, it would seem that Joshua's choice wasn't all that difficult. The good of the whole was at stake. Of course any leader would attempt to root out the sin and restore the nation. Yet many leaders today who are faced with this choice don't follow Joshua's example. They take the road of least "earthly" resistance, and the group often suffers as a result. This very failure to deal with "sin in the camp" caused Israel to spend many of the following years in bondage. Failing to confront sin is also what causes some churches and families to forfeit God's blessings.

If Joshua had chosen to ignore Achan's sin, he would have set many precedents that could have hindered God's relationship with the nation of Israel. People would have seen that they could ignore God without personal consequence, and Joshua would have abdicated the right to discipline others who were living in sin. The authority of leadership would have shifted from Joshua to Achan, because he now would have held the power. If Joshua had chosen to overlook the sin, he would not have been taken seriously as a person who really believed what he communicated about a holy and just God.

As teachers, we must understand the consequences of not holding our students accountable for their sinful behavior. If our students see us wink at sin, it will not be long before they understand that we are not really serious about the truths we claim in our teaching. We give up any spiritual authority we have, because our students realize that our personal comfort is far more important to us than obeying God's mandates. If we fail to hold people accountable along the way, we also forfeit the credibility we need as a teacher to confront them in the future when things get out of hand. If we wish to set an example that will perpetuate a strong faith demonstrated by obedience to God, we must be willing to hold ourselves and our students accountable for our actions.

Joshua understood that leadership was more than simply being a mouthpiece for God. He had to put feet to his words and do the hard work of discipleship and discipline.

4. Establish Personal Spiritual Commitment

Joshua was thrust into leadership as a relatively young man. After he and Caleb came back with the only positive reports from the spies' adventure into the Promised Land (Numbers 13), Joshua's role increased as a companion of Moses and a part of the inner circle that led the nation.

One of the challenges of being placed in leadership is to maintain your own spiritual vitality while expending energy to help others grow in their relationship with God. Often leaders fall into the trap of foregoing the unseen work of personal spiritual development while devoting their energies to building up others in the faith.

Many of the "fallen" leaders we have witnessed in the church world are those who found themselves exhausted from ministry responsibilities. When forced to decide what they would spend their limited time doing, they chose to keep up the "front" while failing to work on their inner lives. This type of lifestyle can be maintained for a while without anyone noticing, but eventually one will become nothing more than spiritual bones much like the Pharisees who were exposed by Jesus (Matthew 23:27).

Joshua learned the importance of submission to his earthly boss, and this lesson was easily transferred to his relationship with his heavenly boss. Joshua remained humble and submissive to his leader over a long period of time. He had many opportunities to bypass the spiritual discipline of submission, but it is evident throughout his life that he was a man who had his priorities right. The evidence of this is seen in one of his final declarations: "As for me and my house, we will serve the LORD" (Joshua 24:15). Even after successfully leading the nation, he was willing to be held accountable to them as he invited them to have a glimpse of his values and lifestyle.

Ultimately, the test to determine if we actually believe the truth that we teach others is if we practice it. The personal decisions we make in the quietness of our private lives provide the spiritual foundations upon which we build our lives. We can make it look like everything is going well on the outside while we are wilting away spiritually. Much of the good that a leader has done can be undone if he or she fails spiritually due to a lack of spiritual vitality.

Follow Joshua's example. Learn from the leaders under whom you are called to serve. Be humble in your response to God and others. And make a commitment to follow God regardless of what others do. When you do this, you will set an example for others who will follow you in the great task of perpetuating God's truth.

Giving It a Try

1. Relying on God for Direction

Few teachers feel a total sense of confidence when they are in the classroom. Even the most seasoned teachers wonder what awaits them as they walk into their teaching stations each session. *Will the students be receptive? What has happened in their lives this week that will inhibit their learning? Will something come up that I am not prepared to handle?*

A key to feeling confident in the classroom is coming to an understanding that God has placed you there and that He will be with you no matter what circumstances arise. God has not called you to a task you can't accomplish. Like Joshua, you can be strong and of great faith when you realize God is the One who is leading you.

This type of confidence doesn't come by accident. We must be willing to submit our teaching to God and His desires. Often the greatest problems arise in a classroom when the teacher tries to accomplish the task in his or her own strength and ability. Teachers who neglect God in the process of preparation and presentation open the door for problems. We would be foolish to think we have the ability to conduct spiritual business through human strength alone.

Each week it is important for you to spend quality time in prayer seeking God to meet your students' needs and to help prepare you to address your students' needs. By doing this, you are saying to God and to yourself that you want to keep Him in sight as you teach the lesson. The great benefit of this is that when a supernatural answer is needed, He will be there to provide it through you. Sometimes that answer will be through wise words, but sometimes God will lead us to demonstrate His love through a gentle hug or an act of kindness.

Joshua was a new leader who needed God. Whether you are a new teacher or one who has been around for a long time, your ultimate success as a teacher will be measured by the degree to which you rely on God as your source of strength. Without God, the best teacher in the world can only communicate information. With God, the teacher with the least amount of ability can transmit truth that will bring life and liberty to a new generation (John 14:6).

2. Recounting Historical Facts

In our "throw away" culture, the past seems to hold less significance than it once held. People often think only about the next gadget that will replace the old rather than valuing the used and making adjustments to it so that its value will be restored. We have learned that it is cheaper to throw away an item than to redeem it.

If we are not careful, this "forward looking" approach can rob us of the foundations that provide spiritual stability in our lives. Joshua was shown by God the importance of remembering past encounters with God. He learned that the future of a nation was built on the foundation of God's faithfulness in the past. Israel would face many tests, and the past victories served as a reminder of how God could provide for them once again. Future faith was built on past facts.

The same principle is true today. Our faith for tomorrow is built on our past encounters with God. If God had never intervened in our lives or in the lives of those we know, we would have no confidence to believe for the future. This is one reason why God grants miracles so much more readily to new Christians. They need to see God at work so they will be able to develop their faith as they mature in Him.

Sharing the spiritual "altar" of our lives with our students is vital. The history of our denomination and local churches is full of stories and examples of God's faithfulness. We must tell these stories to our children and to others who were not there to experience the stories firsthand.

Not only should we tell stories of God's faithfulness to a movement and to a church, but we must not be afraid to tell our own stories of when God intervened in our lives. Ultimately, we must encourage our students to chronicle their own encounters with God so they can draw strength from them and provide encouragement to others. The transmission of our historical encounters with God is one of the best ways to perpetuate God's truth. People enjoy hearing interesting personal stories, so take opportunities to weave faith stories into your lessons on a regular basis.

3. Demanding Accountability

A fact of leadership is that you will have to make hard decisions. A fact of spiritual leadership is that some people who claim to follow Christ will test the limits and will live in sin if allowed to do so. Each of us must ask what we are going to do when one of our students chooses to live in rebellion against God. Holding that student accountable for his or her sin will be very difficult, but it is necessary if your class and your church desire to move forward in Christ.

Sin doesn't remain isolated. Sinful behavior affects others even when they don't know about the sin. Just as when the nation of Israel lost its battle against Ai, many of the things God wants to see accomplished through your class and in the lives of families represented by your class will be blocked.

Joshua was a bold leader who knew how to confront for the good of the group. You are called to follow his example when the need arises even when it is difficult. To do otherwise is to declare that you are more concerned with your personal comfort than you are with the well-being of the students God has called you to lead.

A key to successful confrontation is to have established a spiritual relationship with members of your class before the need to confront arises. Students who know you care about them will be much more receptive to your reprimands than those who have no relationship with you. Also, it is important that the rest of the class understand your motives when they receive information concerning the incident. You can prevent many hurtful consequences of this type of encounter if you have established yourself as a caring person committed to the well-being of the people you teach.

4. Establishing a Personal Spiritual Commitment

An old adage states, "It's not how you start the race that counts, but how you finish it." As teachers, we must keep this axiom in mind. Most of us start out well in our journey as teachers and leaders in the church, but the only way we will be able to stay on course and finish the race strongly is by maintaining our spiritual commitment on a daily basis.

We must avoid the temptation to believe that we are spiritual because those around us think we are spiritual. We must not hide behind the spirituality associated with our lecture stand or the admiring comments of our students. Regularly doing a personal spiritual evaluation is vital. We must firmly embrace the truth that we can do nothing of long-term spiritual significance in our own strength. As Jesus says in John 15:4,5, "Abide in Me, and I in you. As the branch cannot bear fruit of itself unless it abides in the vine, so neither can you unless you abide in Me. I am the vine, you are the branches; he who abides in Me and I in him, he bears much fruit, for apart from Me you can do nothing." We must do those things necessary to develop our own spiritual lives so that when we share with our students, we will be speaking out of a full spiritual container rather than attempting to pour from an empty one.

Seeing those around us failing to take the mandates of God seriously can be discouraging. We may wonder if we are truly accomplishing anything through our ministry. Joshua may have had this thought from time to time. We must remember that ultimately the decisions our students make regarding their faith is out of our hands. Like Joshua, we have a responsibility to determine that we will serve the Lord regardless of what others do. When we do this, we set the ultimate example for our students and others who witness our lives. When we demonstrate that we believe the truth enough to act on it, we are making a proclamation more powerful than any that will ever come via the pulpit or lecture stand.

Make Joshua's commitment to wholeheartedly serve God

yours today: "As for me and my house, we will serve the LORD" (Joshua 24:15).

It Works

I stood beside my friend as he was about to be introduced to a large crowd assembled to celebrate his retirement. I will never forget the moment when he looked over at me and quietly confessed that he must have done something wrong in his ministry. In amazement I asked him why he would say such a thing. His response spoke volumes about his heart. He said, "When Jesus ended His ministry, there was no one there to cheer Him on. Look at the crowd here today. Perhaps I attempted to please man too much."

My friend Roy was not guilty of attempting to please people, but in pleasing God, he became a man who was attractive to others. Roy made it his primary goal to listen to God and to walk according to His mandates. Throughout his years of ministry, he had accomplished many things that would have caused a lesser man to become proud; but not Roy. He remained humble because he realized he could have accomplished none of these feats without God's help. He saw himself as a servant of God and drew his strength from this fact.

I was a young man when I first met Roy. He was nearing the end of his professional ministry, and he invited me to teach a Sunday School class with him. It was a great honor and a valuable opportunity to learn from a true man of God. During the eighteen months we shared the class, I watched him in action as he treated with love and respect all who attended.

One of the most beneficial aspects of my relationship with Roy was the opportunity to listen to the stories he told. Roy was a world-class storyteller. He helped me to develop faith and hope to face difficult circumstances as I recalled his experiences. And he reminded me of how important it was to invest in others as he invested in me. Roy helped open doors for me to walk through that eventually led to the ministry opportunities I have today.

Roy wasn't afraid to confront those in whom he invested, but neither did he use an "in your face" approach to confrontation. He was a gentle man who would quietly ask questions to determine where you were spiritually and challenge you to a greater degree of spiritual excellence. If he saw a flaw in your relationship with your family or with your God, he would share one of his stories and then provide corrective insights. Because of Roy's style and his investment in the people prior to the needed correction, few ever objected to his intervention.

Roy Blakeley died a number of years ago, but his life lives on through my life and the lives of hundreds of others whom he taught and mentored throughout the years. The crowd at Roy's retirement wasn't because of some failure on his part; it was the dividend on the investment he made in our lives. I am thankful that Roy demonstrated the type of spiritual leadership that made us want to follow. I am also glad that Roy made the effort to transfer his faith to us. Now it is our turn to transfer that faith to others.

The Rest of the Story

Joshua's firm action to eradicate sin from the camp pleased God. Joshua went on to lead Israel to victory in a rematch with the people of Ai. Joshua and the people of Israel had learned their lesson. Israel continued to live in obedience while under Joshua's leadership.

Joshua had the fortune of being the person in charge when God fulfilled the promise He had first given to Abraham so many years previously. What had started as a seemingly impossible dream in the heart of a solitary man was realized because the promise had been transferred faithfully throughout the generations. When Joshua finally laid his head to rest and entered God's presence, he must have done so with the satisfaction that he had done his part in perpetuating truth to his generation.

Conclusion

When Jesus came to earth, He related many promises of God. He promised that one day He would return (John 14:3). He promised that He would build His Church (Matthew 16:18). And He promised that everyone who called on His name would be saved (Acts 2:21).

Joshua had the opportunity to be an instrument in the realization of the promises God made to Abraham. In the same way, we have the opportunity to be instruments in the realization of the promises God made through Jesus. We have the great privilege of helping to build the kingdom of God by leading individuals into a relationship with God and by helping them become prepared to take their place in heaven one day.

Roy Blakeley showed me what a true Christian looked like and helped prepare me to be a better citizen of God's kingdom. My prayer is that I will be able to do the same for those God entrusts to my care as a teacher. This is my prayer for you as well.

Let's pledge ourselves to the same or greater level of commitment we see in the lives of people like Joshua and Roy: a commitment to be guided by God in our words and deeds; a commitment to share our spiritual conquests; a commitment to hold people accountable; and a commitment to be in a continual state of spiritual development. If we follow through with these commitments, we too will be able to enter the presence of God some day with the satisfaction that God has accomplished His purpose through our lives and ministries and that we have been faithful leaders.

Personal Reflection
1. In what ways do you allow God to guide you in the preparation and presentation of your lesson each week?
2. What experiences from your past could you share with your students to help them develop faith to believe that God can help them in their times of trouble?
3. What challenges do you face in attempting to build accountability into your teaching strategy?
4. What can you do to increase the depth of your spiritual commitment to Jesus?

CHAPTER 5

Perpetuating Truth Through **Involvement**

What makes Christ's teachings difficult is that they obligate us to do something about them.

~ John J. Wade

When she married her husband, she thought her life would be consumed with caring for him and the children that would come their way. He was a good catch. He owned some land and showed great promise as a farmer. Of even greater importance to this young woman was that her new husband loved God and was faithful to serve Him in every way.

As the years went by, the couple's love grew for one another and for their God. She enjoyed her life because it permitted her to spend great amounts of time thinking about God and praying as she went about her duties in the home. A special connection began to take place between her and her Lord. It was as if she was filled with His presence. People began to comment on her changed countenance.

The woman's life slowly began to change. People began to seek her out because they heard that she was very wise. Before long, her house began to look like a counseling center rather than a home for her family. She didn't mind listening to people, but she decided that she needed to make herself available to the people without her counseling practice having a negative impact on her home. Her solution was to go into the city each day and sit under a tree and allow people to come with their issues and problems. After listening to the people, she would share God's solution for their lives. She began to be called a prophet among the people because they truly believed she was speaking to them on behalf of God.

It was no wonder that when trouble began to engulf the region, the people turned to this servant of God. It had been twenty years since the nation had a leader the people could trust. Since that time, the people had fallen into a lifestyle that was displeasing to God. As a result, God had allowed many difficult situations to enter into the nation's life. The people had experienced enough trouble. They needed God's help to defeat their enemies, and the only way they knew to get God's attention was through one who actually knew Him.

When approached by the people to help resolve the region's troubles, this prophet was quick to come up with a plan. She assessed the region's assets and selected a leader she thought could lead the people to victory. When she approached this warrior to enlist him to lead the troops into battle, he refused the offer unless she would go into battle with him. He knew that he could not win in his own strength. He wanted someone with him who had firsthand experience with God and could guide him to sure victory.

Deborah didn't hesitate to respond to the challenge. She knew this commitment meant she would have to be away from her husband and would potentially put her in a dangerous situation, but she also knew God would be with her. And she knew her involvement would demonstrate her faith in God, which would strengthen her people's resolve.

As she slipped on her shoes and fastened her coat, preparing to go into battle, Deborah didn't know how God was going to help the people of Israel win or what her role would be, but she was confident He would prove faithful. It was her hope that once the people experienced God's faithfulness, they would embrace Him and develop a relationship with Him like the one she had.

Gaining Perspective

The events of the Book of Judges stand in stark contrast to the Book of Joshua. Joshua is a book that begins with a promise and ends with the fulfillment of that promise. Judges begins by emphasizing the successful spiritual leadership of Othniel, Ehud, and Deborah and concludes with the selfish, immoral rule of Samson.

We discover in the Book of Judges that the perpetuation of truth is not automatic. The successful transference of faith requires that those who are entrusted with the faith remain committed to their task of living it consistently and sharing it with others.

All leaders must determine if they will stay focused on the purposes of God for their lives or if they will sway from the course in an attempt to fulfill their own plans. Deborah could have taken the path of least resistance. She could have stayed home, taking care of the needs of her husband and staying out of the fray. Instead, she accepted the challenge God placed before her and maximized it with the strength and wisdom God provided. Deborah was confident she could make a difference through her efforts, and she was willing to make the necessary sacrifices to fulfill God's plan for her and her nation.

Our generation stands at the crossroads of faith. With the proper spiritual leadership, our generation can combat the evil that seeks to destroy us. If spiritual leaders decide to follow the path of Samson and focus their attention on achieving their own pleasures, many will perish and great opportunities will be lost.

As teachers, we are among those who have been given the opportunity to make a difference in our culture. We must ask ourselves if we are willing to make the necessary sacrifices to achieve God's objectives or if we will seek our own priorities.

The decision we make will have a profound impact far beyond our own lives.

Let's take a look at Deborah's leadership skills and glean principles that will help us make a difference in our world.

Gleaning Principles

1. She Listened to People

The Bible introduces Deborah as a prophet and then immediately highlights the fact that she made herself available to the people of Israel as a counselor. Deborah didn't cloister herself in a room away from the people. Instead, she sat out in the open under a palm tree so that the people could approach her and share their concerns (Judges 4:5).

We can find two primary reasons why so many people would seek out Deborah for counsel. First, they believed Deborah had something worthwhile to tell them. It is obvious from her title as a "prophet" that Deborah was known as a person who spoke for God. Over time Deborah's pronouncements proved to the people of Israel that she was no fly-by-night soothsayer who cared more about herself than about the people. Being a woman at that point in history would have presented its own set of challenges to one who would hold such a lofty position in the nation. Deborah's ministry had obviously passed the test and overcome any bigotry that might have prevented her from ministry.

The second reason people found their way to the palm tree was because Deborah knew how to listen. Listening is a taxing ministry, especially when you make yourself available to anyone who might want to come and talk. Listening requires an investment of yourself in the lives of individuals. It is exhausting work, but listening is one of the most beneficial things you can do for a hurting person. Often people receive more comfort from the knowledge that someone is willing to listen than they do from the answers we attempt to provide.

2. *She Was Able to Execute a Plan*

Deborah's ministry of listening permitted her to understand the plight of the people to whom she ministered. After carefully listening to the people's concerns and assessing the situation, she consulted God and received His plan to resolve the problem.

Deborah might have considered herself unfit to lead a group of men into battle, for such a role was uncustomary for a woman. But this didn't hinder her from executing the battle plan. She evaluated her options and called in the experienced warrior Barak to lead the mission. Her instructions were clear. Barak was to take ten thousand men from the tribes of Naphtali and Zebulun to the river and wait there until God brought the enemy to them. Deborah assured him that if he would do this, God would deliver the enemy into his hands (Judges 4:6,7).

Deborah provides an excellent example of a person who could assess a situation, seek God for a solution, and then mobilize the resources to accomplish the task. As teachers, we can use these skills to help develop our students and lead them to spiritual victory.

Deborah's role as a leader wasn't to solve all the people's problems; it was to hear from God and help them carry out the plan He put into place. Leaders in the church today are not called to carry out a battle plan against a competing nation, but we are all called to combat the spiritual darkness that surrounds us.

We live in an era when all followers of God have direct access to Him through Jesus. We shouldn't need a prophet to give us direction, yet many people do need help discerning God's will, especially during difficult times. As spiritual leaders, we have the opportunity to help our students see clearly the path God wants them to take in difficult situations and to encourage them to carry out that plan in their lives. During these times, we can provide an example to these people so they in turn can help others who will one day turn to them in their times of struggle.

3. She Went Into the Trenches

Barak was a brave man and a proven warrior, but he wasn't willing to go into battle alone. He demanded that Deborah back up her faith with her physical presence on the battlefield (Judges 4:8).

Deborah immediately agreed to go into battle with Barak on one condition: When the victory was won, God, rather than the skillful leadership of Barak, would get credit for the victory (Judges 4:9). Barak agreed to this condition and went about the task of recruiting the troops the two of them would lead into battle.

Going to battle is never an easy task. Confronting those who are trying to destroy you always involves risks. A woman in combat had additional risks. But Deborah was willing to go into the enemy's territory to see the plan God had given her accomplished.

As teachers, we can be guilty of challenging our students to do things that put them in peril without first walking into those same arenas ourselves. How often do you challenge your students to witness to their friends, yet you have not witnessed to yours? Do you encourage your students to reject the corruption that is spewed through television, movies, and the Internet while secretly consuming those very things? We must realize that many of our students are willing to walk in the way of righteousness and combat evil if they are confident we will enter the battle beside them.

Deborah wasn't entering a battle unwisely or without counting the cost. She was entering the battlefield with full assurance that her future was in God's control. As teachers, we must be careful not to lead our students into battles that are not a sure thing. This can only be accomplished by being sure that God is the one giving the directions. Leading a group of people into battle against some enemy can be a heady experience, especially if we think we have the natural skills and abilities to be victorious. We must learn from the Bible's many examples that strength doesn't necessarily lead to victory. Victory is assured only when God is in command.

4. She Gave the Glory to God

Deborah was careful to demand that God receive the glory before she went into battle. She was just as careful to give Him glory after the battle was achieved. Deborah's beautiful victory song records the heart and soul of this great leader of Israel (Judges 5:1–31).

Relying on God is easy when you are in the midst of a battle. In many situations, relying on God is the only way you can gain the courage to go through the fight. Being on the "outcome" side of a problem, however, can present quite a different story. After the battle, we may forget about God and revert back to living in our own strength. It is telling that the biblical account of Deborah devotes much more space to her postwar song than it does to the events leading up to the battle. Deborah was a person of character before, during, and after she faced trouble in her life.

As leaders, we must clearly give God the glory for every

victory we experience in our ministry and in our lives. Deborah provides an example of a person who was comfortable in leadership because she knew her role. She was a follower of God who led her people to do likewise. The true evidence of her success was the fact that those she led continued to please God into the next generation (Judges 5:31).

Giving It a Try

1. Listening to People

An old tongue-in-cheek saying among teachers is "Teaching would be great if it weren't for the students." As cynical as this may sound, anyone who has taught very long knows that leading and teaching people can be taxing.

When we are tempted to push aside our students, we must remember that our ministry exists only because there are students who need to grow in Christ. Students pay teachers a high compliment when they seek them out and ask questions that sometimes seem beyond their ability to answer. Many in our society and in our churches simply want someone to listen to them. Often teachers are the people they come to with their problems because students believe their teachers have a connection with the God they speak about each week.

A few tips will help you become a more effective listener. The first tip is to truly believe that people are important. Sometimes we fail to listen to people because we have pressing projects to complete and the endless talk keeps us from achieving our tasks. Our culture rewards the accomplishment of tasks, so it is normal for us not to want to be hindered in the pursuit of those rewards. Unfortunately, the standards of this culture are not the standards of the kingdom of God. God rewards us on the basis of how we relate to people. He says that others will know we are Christians "if [we] have love for one another" (John 13:35), not by how many projects we complete. God's priority is people. When we make people our priority, we will have less difficulty setting aside projects so that we can give people more of our time.

A second key to effective listening is to place your attention on what people are saying and feeling rather than formulating your response to what is being said. Too often people who are in the authority role become so caught up in developing a meaningful answer that they fail to hear the question being asked. When this occurs, the student walks away without receiving what he or she needs, the teacher having done little to help in the spiritual development of the disciple. We must remember that teachers won't always have the answers to students' problems, but they are more likely to provide appropriate responses if they actually pay attention to their students' thoughts.

A third key to effective listening is to realize that sometimes people just want to talk. These individuals don't really expect you to have answers to their problems; they just need someone who will let them share their hurts and frustrations. They need someone to value them enough to give their time and energy. Often these people discover a great deal about their own situation by just having the opportunity to talk through the issues out loud.

A fourth key to effective listening is to attempt to place yourself in the other person's context. It is easy to give glib answers to people based on your situation rather than realistic solutions based on their circumstances. Telling a person to save money each week to prepare for emergencies is easy if you are making a good salary. Telling a person to save money if he or she is living on minimum wage, has no high school diploma, and has eight children to care for is something quite different.

Obviously, this is an extreme example, but often we fail to really listen to a person because the problem seems so small when viewed from our perspective. An effective listener must be willing to see issues from the perspective of the one telling the story.

Listening is one of the most important ministries you have as a teacher. Only when you listen will you be able to address the heartfelt questions your students are asking. Listening is also one of the greatest ways to say, "I love you and I care about you."

2. Executing a Plan

Deborah provided an example of how to develop and execute an effective plan. She first determined that a plan was needed by being aware of the situation around her. Second, she sought God for His solution to the situation. Third, she assessed the resources available to accomplish the mission. Finally, she put the plan into action by mobilizing her resources.

As teachers, we have the opportunity to make a difference in the lives of our students and communities. We often fail to maximize that opportunity because we don't have a plan, or if we have one, we fail to execute it. This can be remedied by following the pattern provided by Deborah's ministry. Let's look at an example of how it could work.

The first step is to recognize that a plan is needed by looking at the situations surrounding us. In most of our communities, there is a great deal of sin and darkness among individuals who do not know Jesus as Savior. The solution to this problem would be for those who are committing the sins to come to know Jesus as Savior. Once we arrive at this assessment of the circumstances, we must either be satisfied with the current conditions or devise a plan to change them.

If you desire to see a change in the conditions, it is your responsibility as a leader to go before God and ask Him for His plan to reach the lost in your community. When I was a child, my church reached the lost through Sunday School contests. God has led some churches to reach the lost through door-to-door campaigns. Other churches have used "phone-a-thons" and big events to reap a spiritual harvest. No particular one of these techniques will work in every church. The technique that will work best to reach the lost in your community is the one God leads you to use. This is the reason why it is vital that you seek God for a plan rather than seeking your answers in the "church growth" section of your local bookstore.

You may feel that as a teacher you don't have a responsibility for such a monumental plan. It is true that you do not have direct responsibility for the vision of your church, but you have been given oversight of those in your class. Some in your class are being negatively impacted by the sin that engulfs your community. To ignore that fact is to be insensitive to the needs of those you have been called to serve. We must remember that Deborah didn't lead the entire nation of Israel into battle; she utilized two families of Israel to accomplish the task at hand. God may be calling you and your class to combat some spiritual enemy so that the outcome will have a positive impact on the whole. If God has given you a plan to impact your community, He has provided resources in your class that can be mobilized to achieve the task.

Once you have determined the plan and assessed the resources, it is time to put the plan into action. As a teacher, you have influence to mobilize your students to action. Students must see the plan, realize the potential, understand that God is guiding them, and realize the benefit of accomplishing a task that will change their world. Once students begin to feel the victory over darkness through leading people to Christ, they will be emboldened to do greater things for God in the future.

3. Going Into the Trenches

For many years, being elected to the position of president of the United States was virtually impossible unless you had served actively in the military. A feeling pervaded the population that only an individual who had spent time in battle himself should have the power to send troops into battle. It seemed somewhat hypocritical to ask young men and women to do something the president wasn't willing to do personally.

As teachers, we are hypocrites if we ask our students to do something we are unwilling to do ourselves. Challenging students to enter the arena of spiritual warfare without being willing to go with them indicates a faith of the head rather than of the heart. If we truly believe God is going to give us victory in a situation, we will have no fear of walking into battle with the troops.

Teachers must avoid the temptation to simply "teach a lesson." Most of us have been guilty of simply picking up the curriculum and reciting the script without first internalizing the material. We can easily say the words, but do we truly believe these words enough to act on them? Until we can answer that question in the affirmative, it is unfair to ask our students to act on the mandates we proclaim.

Some might object to such a broad statement, feeling that we need to teach all of God's Word regardless of our own level of obedience. The argument could logically follow that if we taught only what we were willing to obey, a lot of the Bible would go unexplored.

In answer to this charge, I suggest that it would be better to have the Bible untaught, or taught by another, than to have a teacher challenge students to live something he or she is unwilling to live. Teachers who simply talk about the Bible but are unwilling to live it are a great deal like the Jewish leadership of Jesus' day. Jesus' repeated words of rebuke to these teachers should be enough to motivate us to go beyond reciting the law by living the life that is available to us through obedience to all of God's Word.

4. Giving God the Glory

A student approaches you after class and tells you what a great job you have done communicating God's Word. How do you respond? The pastor compliments you on the growth of your class over the last year. How does that make you feel?

All of us who teach find ourselves in a dilemma when it comes to giving God glory and accepting praise that is passed our way. Some people address the issue by deflecting any praise they receive for their efforts to serve God. Others accept the praise willingly. On the surface, it seems clear which of these represents the biblical response of humility, but this is not always the case. The first can actually be covering pride while the second can be a teacher's way of giving God the glory for God-given talents and abilities.

The true measure of pride can only be determined by examining the heart of the individual. Those who secretly experience the puffed-up feeling pride gives are just as guilty of stealing God's glory as the biggest braggart in the church. Pride is the ungodly notion that I can do something based solely on the abilities and talents I have developed independent of others. As soon as I acknowledge that God is the source of my talents and abilities, I begin the process of giving God the glory He deserves.

Giving God glory can take many forms. Deborah used a song to outline God's worth. Others tell stories, paint pictures, perform drama, or do acts of service to proclaim the glory of God. The secret to telling if glory is truly being given to God is whether the act is designed to build up someone else or to enrich the person doing the act.

As a teacher, you must ask if you teach primarily for your own benefit or to build up others. We must remember that the standard Jesus set for giving anything to Him was measured by what we give to others (Matthew 25:34–40). This principle applies not only to food, drink, and visitation; it applies to all acts of service.

We must remember that our purpose is to give glory to God and to teach our students to do likewise. If we can instill this basic concept into our students and they internalize it, we will have taken a major step toward perpetuating the truth into the future.

It Works

Few would have expected this daughter of migrant workers to amount to much considering her early years. Her father's chosen line of work made it nearly impossible for her to settle into a school or develop friends. By all traditional assessments, young Billie's future did not look bright.

Fortunately, Billie's fortunes were not to be determined by the socioeconomic condition of her earthly father. Her future was in the hands of her Heavenly Father, whom she loved dearly. She was diligent in her devotion to God and sought to please Him.

Billie's desire was to make a difference in the lives of people. She had discovered that education was something to be valued, and she desired to teach people through whatever vehicles were available to her. She sought God to determine what path to take.

Billie felt that God was leading her into the field of writing. When Billie graduated from high school, God opened the door for her to become employed in a denominational publishing house. During her time there, she was able to hone her writing skills and help form the foundations for the denomination's Sunday School program. She also became acquainted with the gentleman who would become her lifelong marriage partner.

Many would have felt satisfied with Billie's achievements considering her humble beginnings. But God's plan for her went beyond the publishing house, and she became a missionary, earned a doctorate in education, wrote volumes of practical literature, and taught in both the local church and university. None of these feats was simple, but she continued to execute God's plan for her life because she knew that through Him she could experience victory and success. Like Deborah the prophet, Billie went to the trenches and acted on the convictions she had developed.

Those who know Billie can't help but think of her in terms of her service to God and others. Her life has been devoted to the development of others. She has always kept in mind her humble beginnings and sought ways to develop the potential in others. In all she does, she gives God glory through her investment in the lives of others.

The influence of Billie Davis's life will go well beyond the years she lives on earth. She has touched the lives of many through personal encounters, through her teaching, and through her insightful words that have made their way into publication.

Billie's story gives hope to all of us who have come from humble beginnings. God is willing to work through the life of any person who will draw close to Him, follow His plan, and dedicate his or her life to that plan.

The Rest of the Story

After the battle was won, Deborah sat back and thought about the victory. So many things had gone right. She easily could have grown proud from all the praise that was coming her way. She even could have started a movement to achieve more recognition and respect for women based on her accomplishments. Instead, she focused on her God and her relationship with Him. A song began to roll from her lips. Soon Barak joined in.

Deborah never could have dreamed that her life would have made such a difference. Just a few short years earlier, she had been simply a farmer's wife, content to do the things that would make her husband's life a little better. Now she had the privilege of watching her nation take a step back toward God. She knew it was nothing she could have orchestrated. God had been kind to choose to talk to her, and she had been wise enough to listen.

Deborah had the joy of leading her followers into a renewed relationship with God. The Bible says that the nation rested for forty years, indicating how greatly her influence had impacted a nation.

Conclusion

The Bible gives no indication that Deborah came from an elite background, had a great education, or was a talented spokesperson. What it does tell us is that she loved God and allowed Him to speak through her. It tells us that she cared enough about people to listen to them. We discover that she was able to see the needs of the people she served and to seek

God for a means of deliverance. And we see that she was willing to get personally involved in the work she was called to do. Probably her greatest strength was that she knew her source of strength and willingly gave God the glory in everything she did.

Deborah's story is especially important for those who lead in the local church, because there is nothing in her life that makes her any different than the average Christian. Each of us has the ability to be used by God in the same manner Deborah was used. The basic requirement is to love God with all of our hearts and to be willing to let Him speak through us. When we do these simple things, people will recognize the source of our strength and wisdom and will be drawn to us as we are drawn to God.

Personal Reflection

1. How do you feel when you know someone is not listening to what you are saying?
2. In what ways can you become a resource to those who are facing trouble in their lives?
3. How can you ensure that what you are teaching is more than words that someone else wrote?
4. What provides you with the greatest source of satisfaction when you teach, and what does this say about your motives?

CHAPTER 6

Perpetuating
Truth
Through
Conviction

*The great danger is not that
we will renounce our faith. It is that
we will become so distracted
and rushed and preoccupied
that we will settle for
a mediocre version of it.*

~ John Ortberg

He had always known he was different. His parents told him that he was born for a special purpose. He hoped that was true, because he had spent many hours wishing he could be like the other young people with whom he had grown up.

His home had been different as well. His parents were much older than the parents of his friends. They had tried to explain why they had waited so long to have a child, but it really didn't make a lot of sense to him.

His family was very religious. His dad was in the ministry and spent a great deal of time in the synagogue. He had temple duty on a rotational basis. It was during one of these ministry times that God had told his dad that he would have a son. From what he had been told, his mother thought his dad had lost his mind.

One of his greatest joys growing up was spending time with his cousins. He enjoyed them all, but one stood above the rest. He had many reasons for forming such a close bond with this cousin, but probably the greatest reason was that they were so close in age. Even though their talents, personalities, and preferences were quite dissimilar, at times it seemed like they were a team destined to accomplish some great goal. One thing they did have in common was a strong commitment to serve God and help people develop a relationship with Him.

As he grew older, he began to dedicate himself more fully to learning about God. He decided that the best way to do this was to get away from society and spend time alone with God. He had heard about the ascetics and thought that perhaps he would try drawing closer to God using some of their techniques. He committed himself to a simple life, determining that he would not spend a great deal of money on clothing and would live in the wilderness enjoying God's creation. He lived off the land and drew near to its Creator.

He couldn't shake the feeling he was getting each time he went to God in prayer. He sensed that God wanted him to go to the people of Israel and warn them that if they didn't repent, they and their nation would face consequences. Over time, the compassion he had for his country and the conviction he had to live in obedience to God drove him out of the wilderness and onto the city streets. He knew he looked strange, but that no longer mattered to him. He believed he had found his destiny. He was to be a preacher—no, a prophet. He was beginning to understand what his dad had meant when he had told him that one day he would be Elijah to the nation of Israel.

John was amazed at the response of the people. Large crowds gathered to hear him preach, but he wasn't sure if they came to see the freak show or because of his message. It really didn't matter to him. He was pleased that they came and were willing to repent of their sins and be baptized in water.

What did cause John a little concern was the talk among the people that he might be the Messiah. John could handle being called Elijah, but this Messiah business was out of line. He knew he wasn't the holy one sent from God to rescue the nation. He knew the true Messiah would be someone to whom he couldn't even be compared. John's ministry was to get people's attention, lead them to change their ways, and baptize them in water. The Messiah would come and baptize them in fire.

But who would the Messiah be? The nation had waited so long for His appearance.

Then, like a bolt of lightning in the sky, the truth dawned on him as he saw his cousin approach. The goal of one day teaming with his cousin to accomplish a great goal was about to be fulfilled. Now everything made sense.

———————

Gaining Perspective

John the Baptist had one of the toughest jobs in all of history. His purpose on earth was to play second fiddle to his younger cousin. He was required to make great sacrifices but never received top billing for his efforts.

The way John handled his situation is instructive to those of us who feel that our ministries are not receiving the appropriate amount of attention. John was faithful to his call until the day of his death. He never grabbed for power or attention. Not only was he willing to accept a supporting role, but he also willingly shifted attention away from himself so that the mission of God might be fulfilled.

John would not have been able to act so nobly if he hadn't developed a close relationship with God in the wilderness. The wilderness was where John cemented his purpose and his place in God's kingdom. Ironically, it was probably in the same wilderness that Jesus spent forty days with God before launching into His ministry (Matthew 4:1–11).

Many teachers resist the "wilderness" experiences that come to almost all leaders. God generally requires a testing time to determine a person's character and convictions. As has often been said, true character is revealed through a person's actions when no one else can see what he or she is doing. Living right is easy when the lights of the city streets reveal our actions for all to see, but making choices no one else will ever know about is quite another matter. Actions we take regardless of the audience reveal who we are and what we truly believe.

Jesus and John came out of their wilderness experience with distinctly different tasks. One was called to *prepare* the way; the other was called to *be* the Way. One was called to a *supporting* role, the other to a *starring* role. One was called to be a *baptizer*, the other was called to be the *Savior*. Each knew his job and the consequences of accepting the challenge.

One of the most valuable aspects of the wilderness experience is the opportunity to come to grips with our purpose and role in God's kingdom. Times of solitude are often when we hear God communicate His direction for our lives. And the words we hear in the wilderness help us maintain our resolve in times of confusion and discouragement.

John emerged from the wilderness knowing that his job was to build a path that would lead people to the Messiah. This allowed him to be satisfied even when the focus moved away from his ministry and onto Jesus. It gave him courage when he faced the wrath of a king. And he was able to continue to communicate with conviction because he knew what God had told him in the wilderness.

Gleaning Principles

1. He Prepared the Way

John the Baptist's ministry was foretold more than four hundred years before his birth by the prophet Malachi (Malachi 4:5,6). Malachi told his listeners that a prophet would come on the scene before the Day of the Lord. This "Elijah" would turn the hearts of the fathers to their children and the hearts of the children to their fathers. The Jewish people commonly saw this preparation as being necessary before the Messiah could come and establish His kingdom. The angel who predicted John's birth to his father Zechariah confirmed that his son was to prepare the way for Christ's coming (Luke 1:17).

People seldom come to know Jesus if they have not first had an encounter with a group or an individual who has "prepared the way." Most people who accept Jesus and remain followers of Him are led to Jesus by a friend or family member. These people provide the seeker with an example of what life will be like for them if they make a commitment to follow Christ.

As teachers, we must understand that one of our greatest tasks is to "prepare the way" for people to come to know Christ and develop a relationship with Him. People who look at our lives outside the classroom must see that the Messiah we proclaim inside our classroom makes a difference in our lives.

John the Baptist is best known for his ministry at the Jordan River. Most who have read the account of Jesus' baptism recall the image of John as a "wild man" wearing camel's hair and eating locusts (Mark 1:6). John dressed as he did because of his commitment to God. His actions and message were not learned from a book. His faith was a reflection of his relationship with God. He was driven to fulfill his call, and it showed in his daily life. People noticed and were drawn to this type of passion.

Little has changed today. People are still drawn to those who have a conviction concerning what they believe. Teachers who are passionate about their faith in Christ carry on the tradition of the prophet in our world today.

2. He Dared to Be Different

People were drawn to John the Baptist's ministry because he stood out from the crowd. The religious leaders of his day were reserved and dignified. John the Baptist was a reflection of the old school of prophets. His presentations were loud and "in your face." He left little to the imagination of his listeners when he shared his message. John's dress and diet didn't make him a better person but did demonstrate that he wasn't ashamed of what he did and whom he served.

Most people want to "fit in." They will do whatever it takes not to draw criticism from others. Children, teens, and adults alike conform to the styles and fads of the day. Entire industries have been formed to set trends and provide cookie-cutter products to ensure that we all feel accepted.

This desire to fit in has had its impact on the church world as well. There was a time when Pentecostals were distinctly different from others in the religious establishment. Not too many years ago, few would have to wonder what type of church they were in when they walked through the door of a Pentecostal church and heard the enthusiastic music, the loud praise, and the sound of speaking in tongues. Today there is little difference between most Pentecostal church services and services conducted by Baptist or Methodist congregations. We all tend to sing the same basic songs, listen to the same style sermons, wear similar clothing, and praise God in a rather dignified manner. The sanitized services many baby-boomer Pentecostals experience are often a response to the negative reaction these Pentecostals received when they were growing up being labeled "different" by critics.

There is no virtue in being odd, but there is a danger associated with the desire to be like everyone else. We soon begin to forfeit who we are in exchange for what others want us to be. When this occurs, we do not allow God to make us into the unique individuals He desires for us to be. We forfeit the opportunity to make the full impact we are capable of making. We also fail to encourage our students to become unique tools in God's hands.

Our world has come to know the Church in much the same way the people of John's time had come to know the synagogue. Many attended the synagogue out of duty and reverence, but the people who needed to experience spiritual renewal were not attracted to these places of worship. Those who had true spiritual needs were attracted to a unique man who had a unique ministry.

People continue to be drawn to those who dare to be different. We must allow God to shape us into the people He wants us to be and minister in a manner that will address the needs of those to whom He has called us to minister. When we do so, we will stand out from the crowd and be used by God to reach those who need to know Him.

3. He Pointed to Christ

One of the greatest temptations we face as spiritual leaders is to place too much stock in our own evaluation of our teaching performance. We can become filled with pride if our students speak highly of us or if our class begins to fill with admiring students. If we are not careful, we can unconsciously begin pointing our students to ourselves rather than toward Jesus.

Despite his great popularity, John never forgot his purpose or his place. His purpose was to act as a path leading people to Jesus. His place was to play second fiddle to the Messiah. Jesus was the main act; John was simply the warm-up leading to the big show (Mark 1:7).

As teachers, we must never forget our purpose or place. Our jobs are much the same as the one John the Baptist held. Our purpose is to act as a path leading people to Jesus and helping them develop a stronger relationship with Him. We never should become guilty of encouraging our students to first look to us for direction. Students must always be challenged to seek direction and strength from Christ.

Our place is to act as servants of the King and undertake in humble obedience whatever He might request of us. We must never be guilty of thinking that our ministry is the "big show" and that in some way we are the stars. There is only one Star. We must never lose sight of this fact.

4. He Considered the Future

John the Baptist spoke and dressed in a fashion that reflected prophets of the past, but he had an eye to the future. He realized that the ministry he was involved in was minimal compared to what Jesus was about to do on the earth (Mark 1:8). John's baptism was designed to reflect a change on the outside of people; Jesus' baptism would transform their hearts.

John was not satisfied to allow his followers to be restricted by his own limitations. He knew their future would be best served if they transferred to another class. They had received all that he could provide. Now it was time for his students to learn from the Master.

John embraced Jesus' ministry even though it superseded his own. He could have become jealous and tried to hold his students back, but he refused to do so because it was not in their best interest. He was convinced that his purpose was to see his followers develop a closer relationship with God. If this meant that they had to transfer their allegiance, so be it.

If John had desired to rebel against God and had sought personal fame and glory, he probably could have achieved it. Satan likely would have offered John the same deal he offered Jesus (Matthew 4:8,9), but John was not jealous of Jesus' ministry. He accepted the fact that Jesus had something to offer people that was beyond his own calling.

God never gives all of His gifts and callings to a single individual. He has designed His kingdom in a manner that requires us to learn to depend on others but not to become dependent on them. God equips some people with gifts that help people come to know Jesus as Savior. He equips others to minister to new Christians and help them take their first few spiritual steps. Others are talented at shaping more mature Christians into the persons God has designed them to be. God has always prepared someone to help our students become more fully developed in the faith.

Following John's lead in being forward-thinking individuals is vital. We must always be looking for what God is able to do in our lives and what His plans are for our students.

Giving It a Try

1. Preparing the Way

I am fascinated by the work done by road crews. Individuals use machinery to dig huge rocks, tree stumps, and other obstacles out of the ground so that truckloads of dirt and gravel can be put into place. Once the dirt and gravel are dumped, graders smooth out the foundation for what will become a road. Metal forms are then put into place so that cement can be poured over the metal rods that provide stability. Finally, asphalt is laid and lines are drawn on the street's surface. The highways that we take for granted would not be available to us if individuals hadn't done the hard work of "preparing the way."

As teachers, we are in a continual process of preparing the way for our students to walk on. We are called to do the legwork necessary to make it possible for people to come to know Christ and to help them grow to maturity once they have formed a relationship with Him (Ephesians 4:11–13).

Teachers who wish to prepare the way for people to accept Jesus as Savior must be willing to live a consistent life and be in contact with those who do not know Jesus. If no one sees the life of the believer, how can anyone be affected by it?

Our lives must stand in contrast to the lives of those who have not accepted Jesus as Savior. Our neighbors and coworkers need to be able to see that the Christ we embrace makes a difference in the way we live. Christians who display the fruit of the Spirit in their lives (Galatians 5:22,23) will draw the uninitiated to Christ. Simply living our lives before those who need to know Jesus is a method of preparing the way to Christ.

Teachers are also called to prepare the way for young Christians to grow. Once again, lifestyle plays a major role. The closer our students get to us, the more they will be able to determine what in our lives is real and what is for show. We must commit to being vulnerable before our students and helping them see who we really are. The more our students witness the process of spiritual growth in our lives, the more likely they will be to follow us along that path to spiritual maturity.

2. Daring to Be Different

Society has taught us that to be different is to be bad. Those who think outside of the mainstream are considered radical. When the secular media attempts to villainize a person or group, one standard avenue of attack is to make them appear extreme. Today's secular media would have had a heyday with the ministry of John the Baptist.

The very premise of Christianity is that we are called to be different from our culture (1 Peter 2:9). Our lives should not be carbon copies of the lives of those who do not know Jesus as Savior, for adopting the world's standards as our own is not in our best interest. Most people who have a strong desire to conform do so because they dread the idea of rejection. This is understandable among those who do not know the love of Jesus, but it is an irrational stance when taken by those who have been forgiven and accepted by God.

No matter how strange we may appear to the world, if we are responding to God in a manner He accepts, we never have to fear rejection by the only One who truly matters. King David's exuberant form of praise depicts a man who was more concerned with pleasing God than being deemed acceptable by his significant others (2 Samuel 6:12–23).

Biblical characters who tended to make the greatest difference in their culture were those whose actions stood out from the crowd. The Old Testament introduces us to a series of change agents who acted in nonconformist ways in response to God's leading. Ezekiel laid on each of his sides for an extended period of time to make a point. Daniel refused to eat the king's food or to bow to his idol. Hosea married and then remarried a prostitute. Esther entered into the king's chambers without an invitation. The New Testament change agents were equally unique. A quick survey of the lives of Jesus, Paul, and even Peter reveal that they were willing to experience the displeasure of society in order to please God.

Don't be fearful to try something new because you are afraid of ridicule. Be who you have been created to be rather than attempting to fit into a mold someone else has designed for you. Your uniqueness is what will draw people to you and your ministry.

Don't be afraid to be you. Let God use your unique personality and talents. You may be ridiculed by some, but take courage in the fact that you will have God's approval if you are ministering as He desires. Like so many before you, if you will humble yourself before God, He will use you, bless your ministry, and make you a blessing to others (James 4:10).

3. Pointing to Christ

One of the best ways to point people to Jesus is to capitalize on teachable moments. These are times when situations arise in students' lives and they demand answers. Resisting the temptation to simply give them the answers to their questions is essential. Instead, we must point them to the One who can give them the answers they need. This can be done through praying with them or by helping them find their answers in the Bible. When we do this, we train students to look to God for their answers rather than to a human.

When our students face issues in their lives, it is tempting to substitute our own wisdom and experience for spending time consulting Jesus. However, to do so is a sure path to destruction for both student and teacher, for the Bible tells us that "pride goes before destruction" (Proverbs 16:18).

Another way you can point students toward Jesus is through articulating the various ways Jesus has made a difference in your life. People need to know that your accomplishments are a result of your faithful obedience to God and following His direction for your life. When you do this, you help students see the value in seeking after God.

We must be careful never to allow our students to become dependent on us. This is difficult when we establish a close relationship with them. We must remember that healthy relationships are never codependent. Reminding students that you are walking on the same path toward Jesus as they are traveling will help them keep your role in a proper perspective.

Many students are hurt when a teacher leaves the church or is directed by God to another ministry in the church. Having some type of separation anxiety is natural for students, but not letting go is unnatural. Don't allow your students to build a reliance on you by your becoming overly involved in their lives. Make sure your students understand that you are their teacher but Jesus alone is their source of strength and comfort.

4. Considering the Future

Inherent in the concept of perpetuating truth is the notion of movement. We are not in a state of stagnation. Our work is a part of an ever-flowing river of life that moves from creation to the new heaven and new earth that await all who follow Christ (Revelation 22:1). We are building the Church on the foundation of Christ through the efforts of those who have lived before us, and making it possible for others to continue to build in the future.

John the Baptist did all he was called to do, but he encouraged the ministry of those who would go after him. Jesus did the same when He commissioned His disciples to go into all the world and reach those He never came in contact with (Matthew 28:19,20). Neither of these great leaders was content with allowing the size of the work he was doing to be the standard for those who followed. They both wanted to see those who followed them accomplish more than they ever imagined.

We must continually challenge our students to be all they can become in Christ. We need to help them identify their gifting and provide a means for them to reach their potential, realizing they may do things even greater than what we will do.

Avoid the temptation to become jealous of those who "steal the limelight" as they surpass you in ministry. Follow the example of John the Baptist, who cheered on his younger cousin as He surpassed him in popularity and effectiveness. When we are able to attain this attitude, we make evident that we understand the true nature of the kingdom of God. Our focus is never on us, but always on others. We desire to fulfill not our purposes, but God's purpose. And God's kingdom, not ours, is the one we seek to see come.

The greatest joy we can have as teachers is to look into the future and see the work of God carried forward. Ultimately, our work is meaningless if the river of life stops flowing. We can take great joy in knowing that because of the forward-thinking teachers who minister life from one generation to the next, the river will never be dammed.

It Works

Jerry knew what the devil looked like and never wanted to return to his clutches. Neither did he want to let him entrap others in sin the way he had bound him as a teenager and young adult. Jerry's passion was to minister to children and young people so he could lead them into knowledge of Jesus and equip them to resist evil before they slipped into a sinful lifestyle from which they might never escape.

Conventional Christians may have considered Jerry a little strange. His background as a research technician trained him to think outside the box. He didn't use normal Christian language; he took the Bible literally and expected it to work in his life, and he questioned the traditions that had become such a part of church life. Jerry was not satisfied with easy answers and refused to be shaped by the typical Christian mold.

Jerry taught the elementary boys in his small church, and he used unconventional teaching methods. He loved to take them on camping trips or into the California hills to gig frogs and look at snakes and other creepy creatures. The boys would always come back with stories that caused their moms to break out in a cold sweat. But they would also always come back with examples of God's handiwork in nature and a deeper appreciation for their Creator. The young people in the church loved Jerry because they could tell he cared for them.

Jerry's relationship with his students allowed him to challenge their lifestyles and behaviors. Often he discovered that it was easier to shape those who had no religious background than those who grew up in churched families. Those children who had not learned how to make excuses for their inappropriate behavior responded well to Jerry's convictions concerning their need to avoid sin. Many also responded positively to his efforts to point them to the Savior who meant so much to him.

Jerry Edmonds clearly understood that the future of the church rested in the hands of the children and young people to whom he ministered. He talked to them with respect, he expected them to develop in their relationship with God, and he challenged them to take part in active ministry to people both inside and outside the church.

Only heaven knows the impact Jerry's ministry had. But one thing is sure: many adults living in our world today know more about Jesus because they learned from the words and life of someone who had a passion for Jesus and a conviction to eradicate sin from the lives of his students through the power of Jesus Christ.

The Rest of the Story

Life changed for John after he baptized Jesus. His entire purpose shifted from turning people away from their sin to turning people toward the Messiah. He was passionate about the potential that existed to turn his nation back to God.

Unfortunately, not everyone appreciated John's passion. King Herod became disenchanted with some of John's comments. Herod couldn't deny the comments were true, but he didn't appreciate the bad publicity. John found himself behind bars with little chance of seeing freedom ever again.

As John sat in jail, he wondered about the future of the nation. At times he even wondered if his contribution would make a difference. He really couldn't understand why Jesus wasn't doing more to bring the nation into conformity with

God's plan. He just had to know what Jesus was thinking, so he sent out a group of his friends to ask Jesus what was going on.

John's passion for truth eventually cost him his life. King Herod's wife became increasingly irritated with John's refusal to retract his statements concerning her morality. When the opportunity presented itself, she convinced her husband to commit a senseless act of murder.

John the Baptist died as he had lived. He was passionate about his convictions, he was unwilling to compromise his values, and he showed people a way of changing their lives if they were willing to do so.

Conclusion

For hundreds of years the voice of God had not been heard. God chose to reintroduce himself into the life of a nation through the ministry of John the Baptist. During the intervening years, a remnant of believers perpetuated truth in the midst of a corrupt religious system. But there came a time when a person of conviction was needed to declare the truth in an uncompromised fashion.

Our society needs teachers who will take up the mantle of John the Baptist. We need individuals who will resist the temptation to conform to the acceptable patterns of society and who will boldly express themselves in the manner for which they were designed by their Creator. We need individuals who will faithfully and unselfishly point to Christ and prepare the way for people to reach Him. We need people who will do their part as a member of the team to accomplish God's purposes. It all begins with a passion for God and a willingness to spend some time in the wilderness seeking God's specific will for our lives. When we emerge, we will be changed, as will those with whom we come into contact.

Personal Reflection
1. In what ways are you currently preparing the way for someone who doesn't know Jesus?
2. How would your ministry change if you shook off the restraints of societal acceptability and ministered passionately according to your gifts?
3. In what ways do you consciously point people to Jesus?
4. In what ways can you encourage your students to do even greater acts of ministry than you have accomplished in your life?

CHAPTER 7

Perpetuating
Truth
Through
Relationship

Little did I realize that my desire to add value to others would be the thing that added value to me!

~ *John C. Maxwell*

He walked slowly toward the garden to spend a little time alone with his father. He usually looked forward to their garden visits, but on this evening he was filled with mixed emotions. The pleasant memories of past encounters were being overwhelmed by the thought of what awaited him in the next few hours. His sadness was increased by the knowledge that this would be the last time he would meet his father like this.

As he approached his destination, he reflected on his time on earth and the impact he had made. In some ways, it didn't seem as though he had accomplished much. He had been a good kid. He never caused his parents grief—except perhaps for that time he forgot to tell them he was going to hang back and learn a little more from the people in the temple. He did pretty much what every other young guy did. He grew to be strong both physically and spiritually. For the first thirty years of his life, family responsibilities consumed most of his time.

But the last three years had been focused on helping people see God's truth more fully than they had seen it before. He felt it was important that people go beyond knowing about God and making sacrifices to Him. He would not be satisfied until people actually knew God and developed a relationship with Him.

But had he been successful in his quest?

Some would question his wisdom in selecting twelve men with such little religious training to change the way the world viewed God. Much of the basic training these gentlemen needed could have been avoided if he had selected twelve men from the religious establishment to work with him. He resisted making this choice even though it had merit. He wanted to work with people who were willing to think outside the box. He realized that in some ways it was easier to teach those who knew little about a subject than those who already thought they knew it all.

But what had he accomplished in three years? He drew a crowd when he provided a picnic lunch, but they all left when he held them accountable for their actions and attitudes. If numbers were his gauge of success, many teachers had achieved more. He had started with twelve followers when he began his ministry. Tonight he had dined with the very same group. What evidence was there that these twelve were any closer to understanding his mission now than when they decided to follow him?

As he reflected on his life, he didn't regret the mission he sought to accomplish or even the destiny that would be fulfilled in the next few hours. He knew he had given his best, and he had to leave the rest to God.

With a tired smile, Jesus turned to His proud Father, who was waiting to spend time with Him.

Gaining Perspective

How do you measure success?

Measuring success on the basis of increase is not uncommon. A merchant judges success by the percentage of increase in sales. A college president often judges success on the basis of an increase in enrollment. The factory boss judges his company's success based on an increase in units produced over a comparable period.

Jesus didn't judge His success based on numerical increase. If He had used that measure, He would have been considered a failure. He had experienced an increase in followers at one point in His ministry, but then He had lost them to other teachers. Some would have considered this a failure, but Jesus didn't. When His life came to an end, His success was measured on the basis of His faithfulness to His call. Jesus came to earth to help people know God more fully and to provide a means of developing a relationship with Him. By those standards, Jesus was the ultimate success.

As teachers, we may become discouraged if our classrooms are not full or if students leave our class to go to another church or another teacher. This type of discouragement need not be a part of the Sunday School teacher's experience. If we adopt Jesus' standard of excellence, we can be successful whether we have one student or one hundred.

Jesus also didn't measure His success on the basis of His students' response to God. He realized He couldn't control His students. They all had to make their own decisions. Unfortunately, not all of them chose well.

In the same way, we must not judge our work on the spirituality of our students. Our job is to help our students see God as loving, caring, and merciful. When we do this, they will be better able to enter His presence with confidence and experience His forgiveness and grace. If we faithfully expose them to these truths, we can consider our work a success.

Let's look at Jesus' teaching style and discover principles that will make us more effective as teachers according to His standards.

Gleaning Principles

1. A Firm Grasp of the Fundamentals

Jesus' ministry was characterized by two attitudes. First, He hated hypocrisy and did everything He could to expose it. Second, He loved sinners and desired that they would come into a relationship with the Father and grow in Him.

Jesus hated hypocrisy because it led people to believe they had to accomplish things outside of their ability. The Pharisees and Sadducees made people believe they were much holier than they actually were. They put on appearances that discouraged the average person from even hoping to achieve their level of spirituality. The Jewish leaders during Jesus' time eliminated spiritual competition by constructing walls that most felt unable to climb.

Jesus wanted people to realize that having a relationship with the Father was not all that difficult. In fact, it was attainable by all people, including the social misfits of His time. Jesus specifically approached Samaritans, women, lepers, and other individuals who had been disenfranchised by the spiritual elite. Instead of building walls that kept people out of the Kingdom, Jesus tore them down so that all might come in.

Although Jesus opened the door to all who would come in, He didn't practice a "love" that tolerated sin. Jesus was very clear about the fundamentals of the faith. People who wanted a relationship with the Father had to first admit that Jesus was the Son of God. Next they had to confess that they were sinners in need of a Savior. Then they had to commit themselves to love God and one another. These fundamentals are not easy, but they are within reach of all, regardless of possessions or position in the community.

As teachers, we must also understand the fundamentals of the faith. We must be very careful not to eliminate people from the faith through a false set of spiritual standards not required by God, but instead keep our directions to them based on the Word of God. Sin must be avoided, but our commitment to our students goes beyond the simple condemnation of sin and attempts to build the individual's relationships with God and others. If our students are developing in these areas of their lives, they will be less likely to be overtaken by sin.

2. A Clear and Understandable Presentation

Jesus showed on occasion that He could hold His own when in debate with the intellectual class (Matthew 12:1–8), but in most circumstances He chose to speak in a way that was understandable to the common person. The New Testament was written in the common Greek, using words and concepts that were within reach of the uneducated of the day. It is no mistake that Jesus' words recorded in the New Testament are rather simple. God wanted the gospel to be accessible to all people so that each person would have the opportunity to make a decision regarding it.

Jesus not only used a language that was understandable for the audience He was addressing, but He also used methods that would clearly illustrate the point He was attempting to convey. Jesus regularly used parables that contained everyday events to make His point. Most of us remember the great parables of the good Samaritan (Luke 11:30–37); the lost coin, lost sheep, and lost son (Luke 15:3–32); the mustard seed

(Matthew 13:31,32); and the seeds that fell on the various kinds of soil (Matthew 13:1–30) because they contain common elements to which all classes of people can relate.

Jesus also used humor to make His point. A common type of humor in the first century was hyperbole (an exaggeration of a fact to catch one's attention and make a point). Jesus spoke about splinters and beams in people's eyes to make His point about judging one another (Matthew 7:3–5). He compared the chances of a rich man getting into heaven with the chances of a camel making its way through the eye of a needle (Matthew 19:23,24). And who can forget the illustration of the gnat and the camel found in Matthew 23:24?

Jesus also used philosophical concepts that were understood by all and then infused those concepts with new meanings. An example of this can be seen in the first chapter of John. The philosophers of the day would often use contrasting ideas, such as light and darkness, to make their points. Jesus adopted these concepts and helped His listeners understand that the true light and darkness represented the spheres of the kingdom of God and the kingdom of humankind. Jesus realized that it is essential to start at a point of common understanding in order to move to a point of expanded knowledge.

As teachers, we could easily fall into one of two deadly traps. The first is the trap of "cultural laziness." This trap occurs when we come to believe that people should make an effort to understand us rather than us making the effort to understand their world. Those generally found in this trap wait for the unchurched to come to them rather than them going out into the world with the gospel to engage those who are not Christians. These individuals feel that those who need Christ should seek Him, and when they are ready to leave their world and move into the kingdom of God, they will be there to tell the seekers what they need to know. Those who are culturally lazy seldom have the joy of seeing people accept Jesus as Savior.

The second trap is the use of "Christianese," the secret language spoken in church and Sunday School that is not understood by those who have not been indoctrinated. Terms such as "saved," "under the blood," "justified," and "redeemed" are just a few examples of words that would have little meaning to the uninitiated. Although the meanings behind these words are significant for Christians, we must be willing to abandon these words when we relate the gospel and replace them with stories and illustrations that will communicate the concepts in a fashion the uninitiated will understand. Jesus used parables that reflected His culture. We might use principles gained from literature, television, and other forms of media that are familiar in our society. Remembering that words are valuable only if they communicate meaning is vital. As communicators of the gospel, let us be careful to choose words that speak to the people of our culture.

3. He Drew the Truth From His Students

Jesus' teaching ministry was broken into two major segments. He taught large groups numbering in the thousands and small groups such as the Twelve, and He tailored His approach to the group He was teaching. When He spoke to a large group, He most generally used a lecture approach, imparting truth to them from His mouth to their ears—the best way to communicate with so many people. It would have been nearly impossible to create a dialog in those situations.

When Jesus taught small groups, He seldom told them what they should believe. Often He seemed to be trying to keep them from easily reaching the truth (Matthew 13:34,35). Instead, He used methodologies that demanded that individuals grapple with issues and arrive at the truth on their own. He guided their journey, but He required them to reach the truth on their own.

Jesus understood that people retain information best when they make the discovery of the material on their own. This doesn't mean that people can determine independently what is and what is not true. It simply means that it is useful for people to go through the process of learning rather than simply being told what to believe. It is the teacher's responsibility to guide the process so that students will arrive at the truth.

Those who have taught realize that they retain a great deal more when they are responsible to prepare a lesson than if they simply sit and listen to a lesson being presented. Something about going through the process of learning makes an indelible mark in our memories.

Jesus used a variety of methods to draw the truth from His students. He was famous for telling a parable and allowing His disciples to struggle with its implications. He often would live out a truth, such as the performance of a miracle or the treatment of a person, and allow His disciples to ponder what had just taken place. He used leading questions and comments, the logical conclusions of which would result in the individual discovering the truth (e.g., John 4:4–26). He used practicums to help His followers experience firsthand the theory they had learned about God and the gospel (e.g., Luke 9:1–6). And He pressed them to go deeper in their faith by challenging them when they seemed to miss the point (e.g., Luke 8:22–25).

As teachers, we could easily fall into the mode of telling our students what to believe. Some things we must tell them, such as who Jesus is, what He did on their behalf, and how to accept Him as Savior. But many things would be better learned through a student discovery method. When we get our students involved in the learning process, the result will be the making of lifelong disciples of Jesus.

4. A Spiritually Responsible Approach

Jesus had the greatest insight of any teacher who ever lived. He had the greatest wealth of personal and practical information, and He had access to the Father that none before or since possessed. Many thought He was the best teacher ever. Yet Jesus was not overconfident about the impact He had made on His disciples. As He was concluding His days of direct influence on His students, He took the time to pray for His disciples and put them in the loving care of His Father (John 17).

Jesus' prayer reveals that He had His disciples' welfare at heart. This is the best example of Jesus praying for His disciples, but we can be assured that this was not the only time He prayed for them. He understood that the enemy was poised to snatch His followers from the fold and that it was His responsibility to pray for their protection and welfare.

Jesus not only prayed for His students, He also entrusted them into God's hands. He knew that He couldn't be with them always. He loved them and was concerned about them, but a time was going to come when they would be passed on to the next teacher. He had to believe that the training and teaching He had provided would stick and make a long-term difference in their lives.

Jesus understood that the best teaching on earth could not bring the results God desired in the lives of Christians. He knew the involvement of the Holy Spirit was necessary to make His efforts effective. If the Son of God understood this principle, how much more should we concern ourselves with involving the Holy Spirit in our efforts to develop disciples in our classrooms?

Giving It a Try

1. Having a Firm Grip on the Fundamentals

Don't discourage students by creating guilt when they don't reach ultimate standards. There are many good things Christians should be doing, but if we are not careful, we can make our students believe that failure to do them will cause them to lose their salvation. Reading the Bible every day is a great goal, but few in the church actually accomplish this feat. Prayer and fasting are disciplines that will benefit every Christian, but we must be careful not to assign spiritual merit based on these activities. As good as these and other spiritual activities are, if we determine a person's acceptability to God on the basis of them, our standards are not much different from those of the Pharisees and Sadducees.

It is vital that we help students see spiritual disciplines as a means of *developing* their relationship with God rather than a means of *determining* their relationship with God. The only thing God requires of us to be in relationship with Him is that we confess our sins and acknowledge Jesus as our Savior. Beyond that He calls us to spend time with Him and love Him as He pours out His love on us.

As teachers, we could easily allow our students to see us as spiritual superiors. We stand before them with answers to their questions and with the authority of God's Word behind our proclamations. This can be very intoxicating and can lead us to do things that we wouldn't do in other situations. We can begin to believe that we are more spiritual than we truly are. Be careful to be honest about your weaknesses, and avoid building walls that separate you from your students. You must live as closely as you can to the Father and help to bring down any false walls that may have been constructed. Help your students gain the confidence that they can be in places of spiritual leadership as well.

2. Making a Clear and Understandable Presentation

We must present the deep principles of the Bible in a clear and understandable manner to have any hope of helping our students learn. To do this, we must be willing to understand our students' worlds outside of the classroom and the things to which they commonly relate. Much like Jesus knowing the basic communication styles and philosophical concepts during His day, we must invest ourselves in the culture enough to be effective communicators.

The first step you can take in this process is to learn what your students are watching and listening to. You may not agree with the philosophies of the material they are consuming, but that doesn't change the fact that these media are forming their frame of reference. Once you know where they are coming from culturally, it is much easier for you to speak their language and to infuse the principles of the gospel into their lives based on what they already know. Jesus did this when He spoke about being born again (John 3:3), drinking living water (John 4:13,14), and guarding the sheep (John 10:1–16). In each of these situations, Jesus used an everyday event in these peoples' lives and was able to infuse it with meaning because He knew what consumed their lives.

The next step in effective communication is to resist the temptation to impress. Too many teachers feel that they need to use the "right" theological term or use words that make them appear to be highly educated. In most cases, the only person this impresses is the teacher. Students don't want to know how much you know; they want to know how what you are sharing will impact their lives.

Jesus didn't try to impress people with His speech. He used the most common examples and terms to help people get the point He was trying to make. As teachers, we must follow His example. We too can tell stories that illustrate important principles. And we can use humor to make our points. We have the added advantage of being able to use video and audio clips from the various entertainment media readily available on the Internet to make spiritual points in an understandable fashion. Granted, some of these forms of communication take more effort on our part, but the connection we make with our students is well worth the effort.

A third step is to go to some of the places your students go and experience what they experience. I am not saying that teachers should spend time doing things that are against their conscience, but if you want to minister effectively inside the classroom, being around your students outside the classroom is essential.

Jesus spent a great deal of time with His disciples. He ate with them, fellowshipped with them, knew their families, and helped them resolve their problems. If you follow Jesus' example in these areas, you will better understand your students' culture and be better prepared to speak into it.

3. Drawing Truth From Your Students

The first step in following Jesus' teaching approach with smaller groups is to understand the abilities of the age level with which you work and believe that God wants your students to learn. Even the smallest child can discover and learn. Obviously, the amount and degree of learning will not be the same for a toddler as it is for a thirty-five-year-old, but many of the teaching principles employed by Jesus can work at all age levels.

Once you become convinced that students can learn and that your primary task is to help them do so, it is imperative that you acquaint yourself with a variety of teaching methods that highlight student participation. Jesus used parables to elicit response from His students. This is still a very effective method today when the stories we tell are open-ended enough to allow students to interact with them.

Many teachers of adults and teens find case studies to be an effective means of encouraging students to grapple with the implications of a principle. Case studies can also be used with elementary children, but because children think in concrete terms, case studies may not be as effective as telling a complete story and then having the children talk about how similar things have happened in their lives and helping them make the appropriate connection.

Another method Jesus used was hyperbole. He said some outrageous things to make people see the foolishness of their thinking. Today we can use methodologies such as the agree/disagree question to encourage students to consider their preconceived ideas.

Jesus asked pointed questions of His followers that didn't let them off easily. When His disciples said people were discussing who He was, Jesus asked, "But who do you say that I am?" (Matthew 16:15). This type of question took the disciples out of the realm of the theoretical and made them decide what they personally embraced concerning the truth. It is vital that we not allow our students to dwell in the theoretical. This is a comfortable place to reside because it demands nothing of us, but it is not a healthy place. Jesus pushed His disciples to do something about what they said they believed. His push caused many to walk away from Him, but it created a small band of followers who perpetuated the truth to our day.

Jesus used the practicum to help His followers learn. You can do the same. Encourage your students to practice what they are learning. When your class is learning about evangelism, set up situations in which they can put it into practice. When your class is learning about healing, take the time to pray for the sick. When your class is learning about the baptism in the Holy Spirit, provide opportunities for people to receive. When your class is learning about benevolence toward the poor, set up situations in which your students can minister to the disenfranchised. Many of these activities can be tailored for any age.

The key to student learning is for the teacher to permit students to discover what the Bible says for themselves and encourage them to come up with practical ideas to put the principles they discover into action. Avoid simply telling students what the Bible says. If they are old enough to read the Bible, let them read portions of Scripture and tell you what each portion means. If they are way off in their understanding, provide guidance through a series of questions that will return them to the correct interpretation. If they are too young to read, read the Bible to them and ask them to tell you what they think the Bible means. In all cases, challenge your students to make age-level appropriate applications to the text in question.

4. Trusting God With Your Students

No matter how good you are as a teacher, and no matter how great the relationship you have with your students, ultimately the effectiveness of your efforts rests with the Father. He alone can birth the scriptural principles in the hearts of your students, and He alone can keep them in the midst of the trials and tribulations they will encounter in life. You have been given a small window of opportunity to impact your students, but it is God who will be their ever-present teacher through the Holy Spirit.

You have a responsibility to pray for your students. If you are not praying for them, you have no right to be their teacher. If you don't care enough about the spiritual condition of your students to pray for them, it seems clear that you see them as an audience for your performance rather than disciples whom you are leading toward Jesus. This is not an encouragement to quit teaching if you are not praying; it is an encouragement to start praying.

Teaching is ultimately a spiritual endeavor. We must always remember that our very best teaching efforts by themselves will lead only to an educated person. When those efforts are combined with the work of the Holy Spirit, the result will be a disciple who will in turn lead others into a relationship with Jesus.

It Works

Mike was a professional educator who had a passion for the development of people both inside and outside the church. He taught at the local university during the week and in his church's Sunday School each weekend. Not all professional educators can make the transition from the academic to the church arena, but Mike didn't seem to have any trouble.

Mike used the classroom as a means of developing others rather than as a stage for himself. He was clear about the basics of the faith, but he had the ability to draw information from his students. Never was there a time when I sat in his class and felt less of a person because Mike held a Ph.D. and I didn't. He respected my opinions, highlighting good insights and redirecting those that eventually would have led to heresy.

Mike used contemporary literature that was familiar to the

class to facilitate the learning process. An example is the series of lessons he taught on developing a Christian worldview. He introduced the unit of study by inviting us to either read or watch *The Chosen,* a story describing the different worldviews of two elements within Judaism. The script was compelling and provided a common foundation from which each of his students could launch. Spirited discussion followed as elements of the script were discussed in light of Scripture and the way we interact with our culture. Not only was the discussion stimulating, but it caused me to reevaluate my previously held views. Much of what I embrace today was adjusted by those Sunday School class sessions.

Mike was not satisfied with leaving us with theoretical information. He held that belief should lead to action. If one's worldview demanded that those who are in need must be ministered to, he was not willing to sit by and not serve. Mike led by example as he became actively involved in the local Habitat for Humanity chapter. His involvement led to the purchase of a large tract of land and the development of a Habitat community that continues to minister to families today. Many who witnessed Mike's commitment to living out his faith followed his lead as they put legs to the theological theory they had discovered in his class.

Mike never put pressure on his students to be something they didn't want to become. He quietly encouraged students to find their place in God's kingdom, trusting God to work through each person as He saw fit.

Mike Palmer will probably never know his teaching's full impact. He has personally touched the lives of thousands of students through his professional and church-based work. He has been instrumental in impacting a community by being an instrument of God's love and compassion. Following Jesus' teaching example, Mike has been a link in God's plan to perpetuate the truth to this generation and those beyond.

The Rest of the Story

It seemed like only moments before the crowd led by Judas made its way into the garden, interrupting Jesus' time with His Father. The time had come for Jesus to face His accusers and to turn to the next phase of His assignment. He knew it wouldn't be easy, but He was thankful for the opportunities He had been given to impact His students over the last few years.

The next hours were a blur. Accusations kept coming. Some were false; others He couldn't deny. He did claim to be the Son of God. He was the Messiah. He was guilty of healing on the Sabbath. He was beaten mercilessly. Before long He found himself hanging from a cross between those who truly were guilty of crimes.

As Jesus hung on the Cross, many thoughts went through His mind. He wondered about the welfare of His mother, about His disciples, and about His Father. He knew that He could be rescued from His plight if He would just call out and request a reprieve, but He wouldn't. He understood that His purpose was to present the truth to the world, and this meant that He must give up His own life so that others who embraced the truth would have everlasting life.

After His resurrection, Jesus' task on earth was completed, but His followers' task had just begun. Now it was their turn to live in obedience to the Father as they had witnessed through Jesus' life. All of the investment that had been deposited in His followers was about to pay compounded interest. The seeds that He had sown into a small band of followers were about to bear fruit that would impact the world until the day He returned.

Conclusion

Comparing yourself to Jesus in any regard is intimidating, but it is especially so when it comes to Jesus' teaching ministry. He was the most effective teacher of all time. Today both religious and nonreligious people quote the sayings of Jesus and remember His illustrations. Most of us would be pleased if our students remembered what we said for just a few weeks.

Although Jesus' ministry can be intimidating, it is not unattainable. Jesus didn't use any techniques that aren't available to us today. He had a clear understanding of what was important. He knew His students and their culture. He communicated in language that was understandable. He drew truth from the hearts of His students. He invited God to be a part of the discipleship process. Every teacher can employ these teaching techniques and can enjoy success like Jesus experienced.

The real key to Jesus' success was that He was more interested in seeing His students develop spiritually and please God than He was about being a success. Jesus was willing to lay down His own priorities so that others might benefit. As teachers, this should be our ultimate goal. When we work toward that goal, God will bless our ministry and do His part to make the disciple-making process we are involved in a true success.

Personal Reflection

1. What do you consider to be the foundational elements of your faith, and how are they demonstrated in your life?
2. What teaching techniques do you use to meet the various learning styles represented in your class each week?
3. What are the advantages to drawing information from students rather than simply pouring information into them?
4. What steps can you take to make your teaching a more spiritual activity?

Chapter 8

Perpetuating Truth Through **Instruction**

*Apart from blunt truth,
our lives sink decadently amid
the perfume of hints and suggestions.*
~ Alfred North Whitehead

He sat in the sunlit portion of the room dictating a letter as his assistant carefully took down every word just as his master spoke them. The master had long since lost his ability to do much writing on his own. His vision had dimmed but not his passion for Jesus and for those he had influenced to believe in Him.

Composing letters to his friends consumed most of his time these days. He had been confined to house arrest because of a misunderstanding concerning his allegiance to the state. What the authorities didn't understand was that he could love his God and his country without compromising as long as he kept their importance in the proper order.

He felt that he would soon be released, but he wasn't one to just sit around waiting for this to happen. He was very thankful that his captors allowed him to have an assistant to help him with his personal needs.

His time under house arrest was far from a waste. To his amazement, he was able to share the gospel with his jailers. Many accepted Jesus as their Savior, and he had the opportunity to disciple these new converts when they came to work each day. Perhaps his imprisonment was God's way to get the gospel into the palace of Rome.

The work he had done before his arrest had been both exciting and dangerous. He had gone from town to town introducing people to Jesus and establishing new churches. As soon as he had begun to be effective in a town, the Jewish leaders would stir up trouble and try to undo all that God had been doing through him. They thought his present plight was a victory for them. But he smiled to himself as he thought about all the benefits his persecution had brought to his cause.

His ministry was exciting because he saw so many people find freedom through a relationship with Christ. But probably the most exciting part of his ministry was teaching new Christians proper doctrine that would shape their lives. He fully believed that the difference between a mature Christian and an individual who would leave the faith was a firm understanding of theology and doctrine.

He learned that working with young Christians is like trying to train children: Sometimes they get it, and sometimes they don't. Young Christians often react in a selfish manner, and sometimes they even fight with one another or lie to cover up mistakes. But the growth he saw in the lives of these people made all of these frustrations worth the effort.

As Paul paused in his dictation, he began to reflect on the last ten to twelve years. He had been stoned and left for dead. He had been run out of more cities than he cared to remember. He had been beaten when he didn't deserve it. Yet none of these sufferings was of consequence compared to the victories God had given him. He rejoiced in the fact that he had been instrumental in establishing churches that still proclaimed the gospel message in Galatia, Thessalonica, Corinth, Ephesus, Philippi, Colossae, and other cities throughout Macedonia. He wasn't quite sure how so much had been accomplished in such a short time. Considering his start, it was amazing to him that God had allowed him to have any ministry opportunities, let alone the chance to make a real impact for His kingdom.

Gaining Perspective

Most Christians have benefited from the letters Paul dictated during his time in house arrest. We have been strengthened by his encouragement to the Philippians; we have been challenged by his call for Philemon to forgive Onesimus; and we have learned a great deal about the Church from his letters to the Ephesians and Colossians. But most of all, we have been able to witness the determination of a man who understood that the only way he could extend his influence beyond his own limited time was by establishing a firm foundation for those who followed after him.

Paul's example is especially important to teachers because of the long-term effectiveness of his ministry. He understood the significance of solid theology and a clear presentation of Christian doctrine. He also understood his own role and importance within the Christian community.

As teachers, we have a vital role in ensuring that the truth of God's Word continues intact to the next generation. This will be done only if we systematically instruct our followers in the truth. Passing on the truth will protect our students from the false doctrines and perversions that compete for their attention. We can ensure the safe transmission of God's Word to the next generation by adopting the basic principles employed by the apostle during his ministry.

Gleaning Principles

1. He Remembered His Past

Jerry was a man who was passionate for God, worked extremely hard in the church, and sought to live a righteous life. I asked him what drove him to live as he did. I will never forget his response. He quietly replied, "I have seen the devil, and I don't ever want any part of him again."

During the early years of Paul's life, he had fought God's advances and served Satan unwittingly (Acts 9:1,2). When God finally got his attention, everything changed.

Even though Paul had many successes as a Christian leader, he had no inflated views concerning his value. He called himself a spiritual "miscarriage" (see 1 Corinthians 15:8) and declared that he was the worst of all sinners before he met Christ (1 Timothy 1:15). Paul understood that he owed everything to God's mercy and grace, and he willingly gave his whole life back to God.

As teachers, we must remember the circumstances from which we were saved. We must remember that we owe everything to God and His mercy and grace. When we fully understand the depths from which we were saved, we too will have the passion to live righteously and to expend the necessary energy to honor God by our efforts, and we will be compelled to share the gospel with others.

We must never forget what the devil looks like. When we get spiritually lazy and begin to flirt with the enemy, we risk a return to our old life. We must flee from evil. When we do so, we will be drawn closer to Christ.

2. He Accepted a Challenge

Generally, in any given situation, there is an easy road and a more difficult road. Those who follow the easy road go to places that nearly everyone has been. Those who are willing to take the more difficult road have unique experiences that often introduce life-enhancing opportunities. Consider the difference in experiences of someone who drives a car across a country versus someone who walks from town to town getting to know the people. The person driving the car catches a glimpse of life along the way. The person who walks the same route benefits from intimate encounters along the way.

Most of the new Christians in the Early Church were willing to take the easier road. They were comfortable staying in Jerusalem or Antioch. The churches in these locations were growing, and God was doing some good things in the lives of people. But when the time came to send out individuals to do the hard work of breaking new ground, Paul and his friend Barnabas were the ones willing to make the sacrifice to cultivate these new fields.

Each of us has the choice of traveling the easy road or the more difficult road. Those who stay and minister to the people who are already in the church are under no condemnation, for the church needs to make sure the truth is perpetuated to its own children and adults. Sadly, not all Christian parents take responsibility for teaching their own children, so a concentrated effort to disciple the "church kids" has its place.

But the church's responsibility doesn't stop at its doors. Teachers must be willing to follow Paul's example and choose the more difficult road. These people see the desperation in the eyes of people living in sin and remember their own condition before their salvation. These people don't care about the background of others, what they look like, or what their response will be when the gospel is presented. People who travel the more difficult road get ridiculed, spit on, cursed out, and thrown out, but they also see miraculous conversions and transformed lives. The potential reward is well worth the risk involved.

What type of teacher are you? Do you like to play it safe and take care of things at home, or do you have a missionary spirit? Would you like to experience spiritual victories that few others have experienced? Take a few steps down the more difficult path. You may find yourself hooked on the excitement this adventurous lifestyle provides.

3. He Valued Truth

The apostle Paul focused many of his teaching efforts on proper doctrine, and he encouraged other church leaders to do likewise.

The Early Church was ripe for heresy. The truth of God's Word was new to most of the people to whom Paul ministered. Many individuals who were only out to better themselves at the cost of others found these new Christians to be easy prey. To ward off these predators, the Christians had to learn the truth.

Many in our churches are no better off than those early Christians. They are relatively new to the faith, and many in our world would like to take advantage of them. Our students need to know how to fend off the advances of philosophies promoted through the secular media that encourage individuals to seek unbridled pleasure through the selfish use of time, finances, and their bodies. The Bible provides godly standards in each of these areas, and it is our job to clearly communicate them so that our students will have the ability to take a firm counter cultural stand.

Paul understood that once people have been taught a principle, what they have learned can become a belief. And once a person truly believes, that belief will cause him or her to change, because behavior follows belief. The things we truly believe and the values we hold will compel us to act in a particular manner. For example, if we believe that church attendance is important to a person's spiritual well-being, no one will have to encourage us to go to church. If we believe that the tithe is a biblical mandate, we will not have to be coerced to give. If we believe God loves the poor and disenfranchised, we will not sit by while the homeless suffer on our streets.

Paul valued truth not simply for truth's sake; he valued truth because he knew it had the power to set people free (John 8:31,32).

4. He Coached People

Paul was not content to simply demand a particular manner of living. He took the effort to coach the person according to the person's strengths and weaknesses (2 Timothy 1:6,7).

Although it appears that at some points Paul had little patience with people who were in the learning process, for the most part we see him taking young people under his wing and helping them to develop as leaders. Paul invested in Timothy, Silas, Mark, Onesimus, and Demas to name just a few of his protégés. Not everyone he coached finished the course, but Paul provided each man with the foundation he needed and the opportunity to learn from Paul's experience and wisdom.

One of the greatest lessons I learned regarding teaching came when I asked a member of a congregation I was pastoring what I could do to improve my teaching. Without much hesitation he said, "You need to stop preaching 'should' sermons." I had no idea what he meant by that comment, so I asked him to explain. He lovingly explained to me that I always told people what they "should" do but seldom told them "how" to do the things Scripture demands.

Telling people what the Bible demands of them without helping them to arrive at that point leads to guilt and self-condemning attitudes. People who find little success in transforming the standards of Scripture into daily living often give up and settle for a defeated spiritual condition. This need not be the case. As teachers, we must take the time and make the effort to put ourselves in the shoes of our students and suggest concrete ways they can live their lives in accordance with Scripture.

Giving It a Try

1. Remembering Your Past

We easily forget what it was like when we were first learning about Jesus. Thus we may assume that our students know a great deal more than they do. Sharing the gospel in a simple fashion is critical if we want all of our students to understand the profound truths of God's Word.

We can no longer assume that children, youth, or adults have heard the stories of David and Goliath, Abraham's sacrifice on Mount Moriah, or even the Flood account. We must be careful to relate the details of each story we refer to in order to set the stage for making the spiritual applications of the principles found in the biblical narratives.

One way to stay in tune with your students is to take a few minutes each week to reflect on how you felt when you first heard the particular story you will be teaching. What was it about the story that made an impact on you? What did you not understand, or what caused confusion? How could your teacher have shared the information in a manner that would have been more effective?

You should also keep in mind the moral and philosophical struggles you faced when you first believed. Perhaps you have been a Christian most of your life and can't remember what it felt like to enter the new world of Christianity. If that is the case, take time to talk with individuals who have lived through that transition and discover some of the things your students may be going through. Be prepared to help lifelong churchgoing students cope with the day-to-day decisions that assist them in maintaining their spiritual lives.

2. Accepting a Challenge

Repeatedly in the Old Testament, the leaders of Israel had to deal with the Canaanites. As teachers, we may think that we have our own Canaanites confronting us in our classrooms. These students seem to swoop in at the most inconvenient times and disrupt our perfectly planned lessons. If we are honest, we have probably caught ourselves praying from time to time that these Canaanites would go to someone else's class or perhaps even stay home.

If you want to be a teacher who perpetuates the faith, you must be willing to minister to the difficult people as well as the well-behaved. Often the difficult person is the one who makes the greatest impact for the gospel once it is engrained in the heart. The apostle Paul is a perfect example of this.

There are a few steps we can take when faced with the opportunity of ministering to difficult students. The first step is to realize that God loves them just the way they are. He doesn't wait for people to become cooperative and well behaved before He loves them. The Bible says that while we were still sinners, God loved us (Ephesians 2:4,5). If we can grasp the degree to which God loves all of us, we will have a better ability to work with difficult persons.

The second step in ministering to difficult students is to realize they can't do a great deal about their condition. Some people are born compliant, some slow-to-warm, and others difficult.

You can tell the easy people from the moment they are born. These are the babies who immediately feel content, sleep through the night early, and love new situations. The slow-to-warm people can equally be identified from the start. These babies do not take to situations quickly; they are a bit timid. As they grow older, they stay out of the flow of activity until they feel comfortable. Once they feel comfortable, they never want to leave. And difficult children drive parents nuts from the start. What we must keep in mind is that such children don't necessarily *want* to be difficult. Their predisposition is woven into their personality. Once you understand that the difficult students aren't "out to get you," you more likely will feel better about working with them.

The greatest challenge in working with a difficult student is learning how to maximize the student's strengths and place the student in situations that make him or her feel a sense of accomplishment. If you are working with a difficult infant, you can provide a situation that is physically comfortable and consistent from week-to-week along with appropriate physical touch even when the child doesn't seem to desire it. Dealing with the difficult elementary student requires the establishment of clear rules, consistent and fair enforcement of the rules, and as much stability as possible each week. These principles also apply to the difficult youth and adult.

Finally, the true secret to successfully ministering to the difficult is to ask God to give you His love for these people. You will never be truly effective teaching students you don't like. We would kid ourselves to say that we have a natural affinity toward all types of people. This is why asking God for His divine love is crucial. He will help us to love the unlovely if we will allow Him to do so.

Drive past the more difficult parts of your city or town and ask God to help you reach for Christ the people who live there. Ask Him to place you in situations in which you can speak to them and demonstrate God's love to them. Go to work as a volunteer in places the "difficult" people frequent or live. As you do these things, you will begin to see these people less as difficult and more as people who have the potential to about the doctrine of Jesus' Second Coming and how this great event provides encouragement, hope, and seriousness regarding their life and purpose. When people understand and embrace the doctrines of the Bible, their behaviors will reflect the character they are developing.

Once people know what the Bible teaches, we can hold them accountable if they begin to live in another manner. Acts of greed, contention, and immorality can be challenged on the basis of what they already know rather than on the basis of an imposed rule. Working in conjunction with the Holy Spirit, we will be able to help wayward persons move back onto the path God has planned for them.

4. Coaching People

A good coach is an invaluable asset to a team. A coach can assess his or her team members and quickly identify their strengths and weaknesses. Once coaches evaluate the individual players, they devise strategies to maximize each player's strengths and minimize his or her weaknesses.

Providing personal examples of how you have put biblical principles into practice is an effective strategy to use in coaching your students. As you relate these stories, share your struggles as well as your victories. But some students need more help than simply hearing your story. They may need you to walk alongside them to provide advice, encouragement, and prayer as they traverse the ups and downs of the spiritual landscape. Don't give up on students who don't get it right away. The difference between a truly effective teacher and one who simply shows up each Sunday is the willingness to go the extra mile.

Being a coach takes a special commitment on your part that you can make only if you believe spiritual development is a